HOW THE GARCIA GIRLS LOST THEIR ACCENTS

Julia Alvarez

AUTHORED by Mai Wang
UPDATED AND REVISED by Bella Wang

COVER DESIGN by Table XI Partners LLC
COVER PHOTO by Olivia Verma and © 2005 GradeSaver, LLC

BOOK DESIGN by Table XI Partners LLC

Published by GradeSaver LLC, www.gradesaver.com

First published in the United States of America by GradeSaver LLC. 2010

GRADESAVER, the GradeSaver logo and the phrase "Getting you the grade since 1999" are registered trademarks of GradeSaver, LLC

ISBN 978-1-60259-233-9

Printed in the United States of America

For other products and additional information please visit
http://www.gradesaver.com

Table of Contents

Table of Contents

Biography of Alvarez, Julia (1950-)

Julia Alvarez was born to Dominican parents in New York City in 1950. When she was three months old, her family moved back to the Dominican Republic under the rule of Rafael Trujillo. Her father became involved in a political rebellion, and her family fled the country in 1960. They escaped just three months before the murder of the Mirabal sisters, vocal opponents to Trujillo's regime, on whose lives she based her second novel.

Her transition to American life was difficult, but she became an avid reader and dedicated herself to learning English fluently. She was sent to boarding school at the age of 13, and she returned to the Dominican Republic each summer. She credits a series of excellent English teachers with instilling in her a love of language and sensitivity to the sound of words. Her 6th grade teacher, Sister Bernadette, asked the class to write stories imagining they were snowflakes or pianos, creative exercises in which Alvarez reveled. Because she learned English as a second language, the musicality of the words sometimes overpowered their meanings, and she recalls repeating words like "butter" in her head for days. The early poems she wrote in English were energized by this initial strangeness of the language.

After graduating from Abbot Academy in 1967, Alvarez initially attended Connecticut College and transferred to Middlebury College in Vermont in 1969. She earned a Master's degree in creative writing from Syracuse University in 1975. In the late 1970s, Alvarez worked as a Writer-in-Residence for the Kentucky Arts Commission. Through the 1980s, she held various positions at California State College (Fresno); College of the Sequoias in Visalia, California; Mary Williams Elementary School in Wilmington, Delaware; Phillips Andover Academy in Andover, Massachusetts; the University of Vermont; the George Washington University in Washington, D.C.; and the University of Illinois (Urbana). Alvarez's first published work was *The Housekeeping Book* (1984).

Alvarez worked as a professor at Middlebury College from 1988 to 1998, and has been a Writer-in-Residence in the English Department since then. In 1989, Alvarez married Bill Eichner, an ophthalmologist from Nebraska and the father of two daughters from a previous marriage. Her first novel, *How the García Girls Lost Their Accents* (1991), was the first major novel by a Dominican author to be published in English. Alvarez also has written three books of poetry, including *Homecoming* (1991). *In the Time of the Butterflies* (1994) was followed by *¡Yo!*, a sequel to *How the García Girls Lost Their Accents*. Among her many awards, recently she was honored with The F. Scott Fitzgerald Award by Montgomery College (Maryland) on October 17, 2009.

Alvarez and Eichner own La Altagracia, a "sustainable" coffee-bean farm seventeen kilometers west of the small ecotourist city Jarabacoa and seventeen kilometers east of Pico Durate, the highest peak east of the Mississippi River. Proceeds from the sales of coffee support their Foundation Alta Gracia, which funds a school on the farm that helps natives of all ages become literate. In addition, the school, also open to foreign students, teaches students about the farm's "sustainable" practices. Alvarez returns to the Dominican Republic and tends the farm.

About How the Garcia Girls Lost Their Accents

Julia Alvarez published her first novel, *How the García Girls Lost Their Accents*, in 1991 at the age of 41. Built from interrelated stories she had been publishing in magazines and literary reviews throughout the 1980s, it was the first major novel about the Dominican-American experience to be published in English. It garnered the 1991 Pen Oakland/Josephine Miles Award and was selected as a notable book by the *New York Times* and the American Library Association. The novel's success gave Alvarez the opportunity to make a living with her writing, and she went on to publish many books of poetry, nonfiction, and five more novels. *In the Time of the Butterflies* (1994), also set during the Trujillo Era of Dominican history, was made into a feature film in 2001. Since then, other Dominican-American novels, such as the Pulitzer Prize winning *The Brief Wondrous Life of Oscar Wao* (2007) by Junot Díaz, have gained widespread popularity. In 2008, the Roundhouse Theatre in Bethesda, Maryland held the world premiere of a stage adaption of *How the García Girls Lost Their Accents* by Karen Zacarías.

In writing the novel, Alvarez drew on her own family's experience fleeing the Trujillo dictatorship. Like the fictional Carlos García, her father was involved in the underground opposition to Trujillo and brought his family to the United States in 1960 to protect them from reprisals. Alvarez modeled Papito on her grandfather, a Cornell graduate who was appointed a Dominican representative to the United Nations. Her mother was the first girl in her family to attend an American boarding school, an immersion in American culture similar to that of Laura García.

Though the novel is not explicitly political, various historical events arise that establish the novel's timeline. While living in New York, Carlos reads about the free elections of 1963, which resulted in the election of Juan Bosch's leftist government. Soon after, Carlos makes a trial visit to the Dominican Republic, but loses hope when a revolution breaks out during his stay. Although Alvarez mentions no specific details, this revolution is likely the coup of September 1963 in which Bosch's government was overthrown and replaced by nineteen months of military rule. The sexual revolution in the United States is also omnipresent, creating a gulf between the liberated, feminist García daughters, and their conservative, "Old World" parents. Although the novel makes only passing references to these events, they form an inescapable backdrop to the lives of the four sisters struggling to reconcile their Dominican heritage with the freewheeling culture of 1960s and 70s America.

Character List

Laura de la Torre García (Mami)

Laura, wife to Carlos García, is the mother of the four García sisters. She is the eldest daughter of the de la Torre family, one of the most wealthy and prestigious families on the Island. Her father, called "Papito" by his grandchildren, was given a bogus post at the U.N. by the dictator Trujillo, who felt threatened by his wealth and education. She attended a preparatory high school in the United States, and she prides herself on her good English and American values. Although socially very conservative, she supports her daughters' aspirations to become Americanized, professional women. However, she has difficulty coming to terms with their liberated sexuality when they are adolescents, and scolds them about using swear words even after they are adults. Above all she is an inveterate storyteller who loves to repeat (and often mistakenly alters) favorite stories about her daughters and family. Her tendency to relate long, detailed narratives parallels the novel's episodic structure and creates a communal history that binds the family together.

Carlos García (Papi)

Carlos is married to Laura de la Torre and is the father of the four García sisters. He is the youngest of his father's 35 (or more) children, 25 of whom are legitimate. Carlos joins his brothers-in-law and a CIA operative, Victor Hubbard, in an unsuccessful coup to overthrow the Dominican dictator Trujillo. Although never captured or imprisoned, he is constantly under suspicion by the *guardia*, the secret police of the Island. Eventually he flees with his family to New York, and as news of the political situation back home worsens, he settles in as an American resident. He is a well-respected doctor and opens a successful medical practice in the Bronx. Although he seems to regret having no sons, he likes to say, "Good bulls sire cows," and he is a devoted father to his daughters. However, his social conservatism and patriarchal convictions contribute to considerable strife between himself and his Americanized, feminist daughters.

Carla García

The eldest of the four sisters, Carla was around 12 when the family moved to the United States, and had great difficulty adjusting to the new country. Her disturbing experience of going through puberty in an alien—and sometimes hostile—culture may have contributed to her decision to become a child psychologist. She is married to the analyst she began seeing when her first marriage fell apart, and often speaks to him in psychology jargon that irritates her younger sisters.

Sandra García (Sandi)

The second eldest sister, Sandra, is fair-haired, light-skinned, and blue-eyed, traits she inherited from a Swedish ancestor, and which distinguish her in the family. A keen observer of power dynamics, she recognizes her beauty as a tool that will gain her acceptance in American culture. However, she is a deeply dissatisfied person, haunted by a gnawing emptiness that cannot be filled by beauty, lovers, scholarship awards, or work. She becomes obsessed with weight loss and suffers a nervous breakdown in graduate school, for which she is temporarily committed to a private mental hospital.

Yolanda García (Yo, Yoyo, Joe)

Yolanda, the third daughter, is a teacher by profession but a poet at heart. She narrates much of the novel, including the opening and closing chapters, and is sensitive to the power and sound of language. She explores the materiality of words, often speaking in rhyme and using surreal images, and defines her romantic relationships based on her partner's relationship to language. She has a nervous breakdown during her first marriage and is committed to a private mental hospital where she suffers an "allergic reaction" to words like "love" and "alive." Her stories are often attempts to understand what fears, desires and personality traits have caused her romantic relationships to fail.

Sofía García (Fifi)

Known as the "maverick" of the family, the youngest daughter Sofía drops out of college and is the only girl without an advanced degree. She runs away from home to elope with her husband, a German chemist named Otto whom she met on the street in Colombia. Despite her rebellious, apparently aimless youth, she is the only daughter with children, no divorces, and a healthy family life when the novel opens. The family considers her the most fiercely independent of the four girls.

The Fannings

Dr. and Mrs. Fanning are a wealthy American couple who arrange Carlos García's fellowship at an American hospital in order to get the family safely out of the Dominican Republic. Dr. Fanning is a famous surgeon who visited the Dominican Republic to teach new heart surgery procedures to the country's prominent doctors. His wife Sylvia is a lively, somewhat crass woman who makes a suggestive overture to Carlos.

Manuel Gustavo

Manuel Gustavo is the illegitimate son of Tío Orlando, one of Carlos's brothers. Tío Orlando hides the infidelity from his wife by passing Manuel off as the son of Tío Ignacio, a bachelor whom the family suspects is homosexual. Manuel and Sofía date during the year Sofía spends in the Dominican Republic. Sofía is devoted to him, but her sisters find him repulsively macho, misogynist and willfully ignorant. He tries to control Sofía's clothing and appearance, reading material, and so on. Worse, he refuses to wear condoms, which he believes cause infertility. Sofía's sisters fear that she will become pregnant and be forced to marry him, so they plot to break up the relationship.

Victor Hubbard

An American from Indiana and a pedophile, Victor Hubbard attended Yale with Tío Mundo before joining the CIA. His position of American consul in the Dominican Republic is a front for his mission to overthrow the dictator Trujillo. When the U.S. State Department withdraws its support from the failed coup, Victor dedicates himself to getting all of the conspirators out of the country safely, including Carlos García.

Papito and Mamita

Laura's parents, called Papito and Mamita by their children and grandchildren, are the oldest living de la Torres. Their full names are Don Edmundo Antonio de la Torre and Doña Yolanda Laura María Rochet de la Torre. Papito holds a bogus post at the United Nations that requires him to visit New York often. The dictator Trujillo conferred the post on him to keep him out of the country, considering his wealth and education a threat to the regime. However, Papito is a peaceable and quiet man, often dominated by his demanding wife, a once-beautiful woman who has become an anxious and self-involved hypochondriac in her old age.

Chucha

Chucha, a Haitian woman who practices voodoo, has served the de la Torre family since before Laura's birth. She appeared one night on Papito and Mamita's doorstep begging asylum after having escaped a massacre of Haitians ordered by Trujillo. The other servants fear her and the spirits she claims to summon, so she has her own room in the house, where she sleeps in her coffin to prepare herself for death. She is left to tend the vacant house after the Garcías flee the Island for the United States.

Major Themes

Storytelling

Characters in the novel, especially the girls' mother Laura, love to tell stories. Unlike straightforward facts, stories allow the listener to immerse him or herself in the life of an individual or a given moment, absorbing emotional information that would otherwise be lacking. Stories also reveal much abo⸺ ⸺toryteller. By structuring the novel as a series of stories about each ⸺ ⸺netimes with characters telling stories within stories, Alvarez ⸺ ⸺ents in the García family's life, but also how the chara⸺ ⸺ shaped by those events.

The chapter "The Four Girls" sho⸺ ⸺elling stories to diverse audiences. The chapter esta⸺ ⸺ytelling and demonstrates how shared stories exp⸺ ⸺diosyncrasies and create a communal history that binds those indi⸺ ⸺to a family. Her stories also reveal her own values and attitudes. As Laura narrates the development of Sandra's nervous breakdown to Dr. Tandlemann, she unknowingly conveys her own inability to understand her daughter's struggle, alerting the doctor and the reader to her inadvertent role in Sandra's troubles. Likewise, her sanitized version of Sofía's elopement suggests the rigid morality from which Sofía fled in the first place.

Carla, as a child psychologist, treats stories as puzzles to be analyzed for clues about the subject's later development. The other sisters also look for traces of their mature selves in their stories. Sandra's stories, for instance, point to trivial instances of dissatisfaction that indicate an underlying cause of her nervous breakdown. Yolanda explains that she tells the Rudy Elmenhurst story to help herself understand why her relationship with Rudy failed. Yolanda also closes the novel by musing over whether her art—the art of storytelling—might derive from lingering childhood guilt. As a child, when her inarticulate feelings and intuitions took shape as images, she was haunted by visions of a black mother cat whose kitten she had stolen. The cat becomes an emblem for Yolanda's life of anxiety, insomnia and bad dreams—psychological disturbances that compel her to tell stories a means of picking apart her past and trying to understand herself. This seemingly disconnected final chapter thus represents a final stage in Yolanda's struggle to locate the roots of her compulsion to write. Her discovery marks the impetus behind the novel's scattered structure by showing how the act of storytelling can help the storyteller (in this case, the novel's characters themselves) find meaning and patterns in the jumble of events that compose a life.

Patriarchy and Machismo

Two forms of patriarchy dominate the novel: the traditional Dominican family structure and the tyrannical dictatorship of Rafael Trujillo. For the four García sisters, the United States becomes a haven from both forms of oppression. Just as the family flees to the States seeking safety from Trujillo's police state, so the daughters venture into the freedoms of American feminism and the sexual revolution of the 1960s.

Although initially forced to move to the United States, the girls soon absorb American culture and voluntarily embrace American teenage life. Once they have a taste for feminism and sexual freedom, they begin to see the Dominican Republic as a tunnel in which people blindly accept unjust traditions. The girls attempt to preach about feminism, Susan B. Anthony and Virginia Woolf to their aunts and cousins, but these relatives prefer the upper-class Dominican woman's life of refinement and leisure to pursuing ideals of freedom. In fact, the same itch for freedom that allows the four García sisters to lead full lives in the United States might have led them to sacrifice themselves for political liberty in the Dominican Republic. Three months after Julia Alvarez's own family escaped the Dominican Republic, three sisters who opposed Trujillo's dictatorship were murdered. The specter of "what could have been" thus lurks behind the novel.

The novel makes the parallel between private and political despotism explicit in the chapter "A Regular Revolution." In this chapter, he girls notice that their plot to break up Sofía's relationship with her domineering Dominican boyfriend is carried out on the same avenue where the Trujillo was ambushed on his way to visit his mistress. Their father's involvement in the failed coup had forced the family to flee the country. Now the sisters hope to drive Sofía from the country a second time, for fear that an unwanted pregnancy will compel her to marry her boyfriend and become a victim of Dominican paternalistic society.

In another scene, Yolanda, a ninth-grader beginning to adjust to American life, writes a speech inspired by Whitman. Her father tears up the "disrespectful" speech and Yolanda retaliates by calling him Trujillo's hated nickname "Chapita." Yolanda immediately regrets the unwise comparison, but Carlos is apparently disturbed by the suggestion that he could become, in his personal life, the very thing he hated in the political sphere. The next day he buys Yolanda a new typewriter and explains that he only wants to protect her. This paternalistic protection, however, may be only a gentler form of the same masculine urge to control.

Indeed, Carlos cannot shake free of his paternalism. By the time he turns 70, he recognizes that he alone of his family has been unable to integrate into American society. His professional, educated daughters and his resourceful wife do not depend on him as women are expected to in Dominican culture. He thinks in economic terms, however, not imagining how his role as their father might extend beyond material support. He fails to see how his urge to assert masculine dominance has excluded him from his daughters' growth.

Sexuality

The girls must adapt to American culture and to their maturing bodies at the same time. Carla, the eldest, is twelve when the family moves to the United States, and is teased cruelly at school for her accent and changing body. Her sisters have more time to absorb English and American culture before undergoing puberty, but their sexual identities are likewise shaped by their immigrant background. In college, Yolanda's discomfort with her sexuality parallels the stiff formality with which she treats English, and she wishes she could act and speak as casually as the other students who have no divided cultural loyalties.

While the girls struggle to fit into a foreign society and new bodies, they must conceal their sexual activity from their parents. The four girls come of age during the sexual revolution in 1960s and 70s America, when feminism encouraged women to take control of their bodies and pursue sexual pleasure uninhibited by cultural prejudices. This attitude differs dramatically from the machismo and emphasis on female virginity in Dominican culture. These conflicting sets of sexual values are a principal source of controversy between the four feminist, Americanized daughters and their conservative parents.

Language

Language, a fundamental marker of social belonging, plays a crucial role in the daughters' lives and identities as Dominican immigrants growing up in the United States. Spanish and English imply different cultural contexts: for example, as teenagers, the girls switch from "Mami" to "Mom" when they want their mother to feel that she has failed them as an American-style parent.

At the novel's opening, the adult sisters are more comfortable with English than with Spanish. As it moves back in time, however, the novel reveals their initial struggle with this alien language in which racial slurs and crude terms are hurled at them. When they first immigrate, language and sexuality are the two most troubling aspects of their cultural displacement. Since the girls undergo puberty soon after immigrating to the States, they learn sexual terms in English before Spanish, and their discomfort with English contributes to their confusion about their new bodies.

Yolanda, as a poet and the novel's primary narrator, has the closest and most troubled relation to language. Because she learns English as a second language, Yolanda develops sensitivity to the musicality of the words. She searches for a romantic partner who treats language with reverence, but without much success. The intensity of Yolanda's relation to language nurses an uneasy relativism in her, and she resists the idea that the outside world is more "real" or meaningful than her surreal poetic visions.

Family

The Garcías' fundamental belief in the importance of family keeps them unified despite their strong, divergent personalities and sometimes contradictory convictions. Dominican family structure conforms to a rigid hierarchy intended to preserve the family honor and the power of the family patriarch. Carlos's concern with how his daughters' sexuality reflects on his name and reputation derives from this traditional structure. Since family ties determine social status, cousins often marry each other to keep money and influence from passing out of the family. The García girls resent this hierarchical system, but the Dominican attitude toward family keeps the de la Torre clan, and the six Garcías, closely knit. This Dominican value of family unity remains intact even as the girls pursue an American vision of individuality and personal independence.

Rebellion

Private and political rebellions play a crucial role in the García sisters' lives. Their father's rebellion against Trujillo's oppressive dictatorship brings them to the United States, where the sexual revolution of the 1960s and 70s awakens the girls' own spirit of rebellion and independence. Their rebellion is spurred by American ideals of personal growth and individual liberties, values that sometimes conflict with the set hierarchies of Dominican society. In the American cultural milieu of the time, feminism encouraged uninhibited sexual exploration, trends towards which the strong, ambitious García sisters are drawn.

Ironically, their father does not recognize the parallel between his political activities and his daughters' desire for personal freedom. His daughters, however, make this parallel explicit in various ways. The three older girls notice that their plan to free Sofía from her tyrannical Dominican boyfriend is carried out on the same avenue where conspirators attacked the Trujillo, in a plot partly organized by their father. On another occasion, Yolanda calls her father by Trujillo's hated nickname after he tears up her defiant, Whitman-inspired speech.

Also ironically, the most rebellious and promiscuous daughter, Sofía, is the only girl with a settled, fulfilling family life in the time covered by the novel. She shakes off the demands of upwardly mobile, materialistic American society by dropping out of college, and violates loyalties central to Dominican culture by running away and eloping. Yet her fiercely independent spirit helps her find satisfaction and happiness in her own way. Rebellion thus appears destructive and generative at the same time, breaking down accepted codes and driving characters to open new, sometimes frightening possibilities.

Creativity

The members of the García family are creative and resourceful, qualities that enable them to adapt and flourish in a new country (as Chucha, their Haitian maid, predicts). The novel explores various forms of creativity, including the less obvious examples of using nail polish to create makeshift red sneakers or finding ways to dodge parental restrictions and sneak out to parties, football games, dates with boys and so on. Even Laura finds creative outlets for her immense energy, initially by inventing improved household devices, then by seeking ways to contribute to her husband's medical clinic and by taking adult classes in business and real estate.

Sandra's and Yolanda's stories suggest how creativity may be either nurtured or crushed in a child. Both girls have active imaginations that create vivid internal worlds that the girls yearn to express. They envision their creative energy taking the shape of animals such as birds or cats that strive to be liberated into the external world, whether through drawing or poetry. As young girls, their creativity is compulsive and untamed, transforming the world around them into a strange, lively place. Sandra sees Doña Charito's tongue as a fat purple horse and brings the hummingbirds on her shirt to life, while Yolanda imagines spirits haunting the coal shed. Unfortunately, a broken arm causes Sandra to be isolated and pampered for a number of months as a child. In that time, she becomes dependent on her mother's attention and external affirmation, and loses her urge to explore her own imagination. Yolanda, by contrast, retreats increasingly into the surreal universe she weaves in her mind using language. Oddly, Sandra's lost imagination seems to contribute to the inner emptiness that causes her breakdown, while Yolanda's breakdown is precipitated by the very intensity of her inner world, which she does not always distinguish from external reality.

Glossary of Terms

Acclimate

to adapt to a new environment, situation or climate

Amorous

in love; stirred by loving or sexual feelings

Balk

to resist carrying out an action

Batten

to fasten down, in preparation for a disruptive event

Bumpkin

someone awkward or unsophisticated, from a rural area

Cotillion

a ballroom dance for couples involving frequent changing of partners

Cowed

intimidated, subdued

Euphemism

an agreeable word substituted for a potentially offensive or unpleasant term

Gossamer

very light, delicate, sometimes translucent (often applied to fabrics)

Hackneyed

clichéd, lacking freshness or originality

Imbibe

to drink, consume liquid

Impotence

the inability to conceive children due to a failure of the functioning of sexual organs

Incongruous

not conforming to the surrounding pattern, lacking harmony or propriety

Maverick

an independent-minded person who does not follow a group or faction

Orifice

an opening, such as a vent, hole, or mouth, through which something may pass

Proviso

a conditional stipulation (as in a contract or legal agreement)

Pungent

giving off an intense, often sharp or acrid flavor or odor

Reminisce

to think back on the past, to discuss old memories

Tryst

an appointed meeting, often between illicit lovers

Tycoon

businessperson with exceptional wealth and power

Vivacious

lively, energetic or high-spirited

Short Summary

The novel is structured episodically as a series of interrelated stories told in reverse chronological order. Part 1 begins with the adult lives of the sisters between 1989 and 1972. In the first chapter, "Antojos," Yolanda visits her family in Dominican Republic as an adult and interacts with people from high and low social classes. Chapter 2, "The Kiss," brings the other three sisters into the picture and establishes their close relationship to each other and the difficulty they have had reconciling their American brand of feminism and sexual liberation with their parents' conservatism. This chapter focuses on the free-spirited Sofía as she plans a 70th birthday party for her father, from whom she has been estranged since she eloped six years ago. Chapter 3, "The Four Girls," relates stories told about each girl by their mother in different situations, demonstrating how storytelling binds the family together through a shared history. The last chapter of Part 1, "The Rudy Elmenhurst Story," tells the story of Yolanda's first serious relationship and her trouble integrating during her first year at a co-ed college.

Part 2 takes place between 1970 and 1960 and centers on the family's experience as recent immigrants to the United States. Chapter 6, "A Regular Revolution," describes how quickly the girls adjust to the freedoms of teenage life in the States after their initial discomfort. When their mother discovers a baggy of marijuana in their house, Sofía claims it as hers and agrees to spend a year in the Dominican Republic. When the family visits her a few months later, the sisters are shocked at how thoroughly she has absorbed Dominican culture, including its emphasis on dolled-up femininity and strutting machismo. They scheme to split up her relationship with her tyrannically misogynistic cousin, Manuel Gustavo. "Daughter of Invention" relates how Yolanda and her mother simultaneously search for creative outlets and personal growth as they begin adapting to their new culture. Her mother spends hours inventing improved devices, until one day she discovers that her idea for a rolling suitcase has just been patented by someone else. Yolanda begins to write poems in her new language, and she is asked to deliver an address for a teacher appreciation day in ninth grade. Her initial attempt at a rebellious speech, inspired by Whitman, enrages her conservative father. In "Trespass," Carla recalls a traumatic encounter with a pervert on her walk home from school, where she is regularly bullied by racist boys. The brief ninth chapter, "Snow," is about Yolanda's first snowfall, which she mistakes for the radioactive dust she has been warned will fall in an atomic explosion. The final chapter of this section, "Floor Show," takes place at a Spanish restaurant in New York, where the Garcías are being treated to a welcome dinner by a prominent American doctor and his wife. The childless couple helped Carlos secure the fellowship that brought him to the United States, and are now working to find him gainful employment. The episode is narrated by Sandra, who is beginning to understand the power of her good looks, and is shocked to see the doctor's drunken wife kiss Carlos on the lips.

The girls' childhood in the Dominican Republic between 1960 and 1956 forms the novel's final section. "The Blood of the Conquistadores" narrates the family's last day on the Island before fleeing hurriedly to the United States. Two thugs from the secret police enter the house to interrogate Carlos, who is under suspicion after helping to plan a failed coup against the dictator Trujillo. Carlos hides in a secret room until a CIA agent who fronts as the American consul, Victor Hubbard, intervenes and whisks the family to the airport. The chapter is narrated from many perspectives, including those of Carlos, their Haitian maid Chucha, the pedophilic CIA agent Victor Hubbard, a brothel madam, and even one of the secret police, capturing a wide range of Dominican voices and characters. In the next chapter, "The Human Body," Yolanda relates an episode from her childhood in which she agrees to show her friend Mundín her private parts if he will give her a large coil of pink clay he received as a gift. Yolanda's childish curiosity and creativity are contrasted implicitly with the masculine brutality of the dictator Trujillo, who marches his young grandson around in a military uniform. "Still Lives" explores Sandra's early artistic talent and the ways creativity may be nurtured or frozen in a child. Sandra's gift vanishes after an encounter with an apparently insane master sculptor leaves her with a broken arm; as an invalid, she is isolated and pampered, conditions that stunt her independent spirit. In "An American Surprise," the girls receive mechanized banks from New York for Christmas. Carla gives her bank, a statuette of the Virgin Mary ascending, to a superstitious servant who is dismissed on suspicion of having stolen it. The truth emerges too late, and the story reveals the unsentimental reality of Dominican class relations and the conflation of Christianity with voodoo-like superstition by the lower classes. Yolanda narrates the final chapter, "The Drum," about a drum she receives for Christmas, and in which she hides a kitten she pilfered from its mother. Yolanda ends up throwing the kitten out of a window in fear, and is then haunted by visions of the mother cat for months and even years after. In the novel's final paragraph, Yolanda hints that her creative life—including her poetry and storytelling—is driven by some residue of the guilt and terror of this experience.

Quotes and Analysis

During his two visits, the grandfather had stood guard by the crib all day, speaking to little Carlos. "Charles the Fifth; Charles Dickens; Prince Charles." He enumerated the names of famous Charleses in order to stir up genetic ambition in the boy. "Charlemagne," he cooed at him also, for the baby was large and big-boned with blond fuzz on his pale pink skin, and blue eyes just like his German father's. All the grandfather's Caribbean fondness for a male heir and for fair Nordic looks had surfaced. There was now good blood in the family against a future bad choice by one of its women.

How the GarcÃ−a Girls Lost Their Accents, pgs. 26-27

This passage describes Carlos's reaction to his grandson, Sofía's son, also named Carlos, who is the first male born to the family in two generations. The elder Carlos had been estranged from his youngest daughter Sofía after she eloped with a German man six years ago, and has only reconciled with her since the birth of her son. Sofía is offended by her father's "macho baby-talk," especially since he does not lavish such attention on Sofía's four-year-old daughter. Here, the narrator takes an ironic tone, describing Carlos as standing "guard" to hint at his excessive devotion; similarly, the word "enumerate" suggests Carlos's undue pomp. Even the series of great men seems absurd when described as a list of "Charleses," an amusingly awkward term that indicates how little these men truly have in common with each other, or with the newborn baby. While Carlos is overjoyed that his name will be perpetuated in the United States, the passage's tone suggests that his pride in masculinity and naming is misplaced. The last line of the passage reveals how deep the misogyny and racial hypocrisy runs in the Dominican family system. The statement implies that a woman will tarnish the family honor by marrying a darker man below her station: the baby's Germanic blood will protect the family by lightening the skin of all his descendants.

"I don't want loose women in my family," he had cautioned all his daughters. Warnings were delivered communally, for even though there was usually the offending daughter of the moment, every woman's character could use extra scolding.

The daughters had had to put up with this kind of attitude in an unsympathetic era. They grew up in the late sixties. Those were the days when wearing jeans and hoop earrings, smoking a little dope, and sleeping with their classmates were considered political acts against the military-industrial complex. But standing up to their father was a different matter altogether. Even as grown women, they lowered their voices in their father's earshot when alluding to their bodies' pleasure. Professional women, too, all three of them, with degrees on the wall!

The narrator looks back on Carlos' repeated warnings to his daughters about maintaining their virginity during high school and college. The passage comes just after the birth of Sofía's son and reflects with some amusement on the daughters' continued lip service to their father's outmoded values, despite having grown into independent, sexually active adults. This conflict between their parents' conservative Dominican values and the cultural mores of the American 1960s is central to the García sisters' struggle to reconcile the two halves of their Dominican-American identity. While trying to blend into American teenage liberation, they must temper their urge towards independence and feminism with respect for a radically different cultural ideal. Their parents' adherence to traditional patriarchy is so strong that even the three eldest girls' advanced degrees and independent incomes cannot shake their father's preoccupation with their chastity.

Supposedly, the parents were heavy-duty Old World, but the four daughters sounded pretty wild for all that. There had been several divorces among them, including Yolanda's. The oldest, a child psychologist, had married the analyst she'd been seeing when her first marriage broke up, something of the sort. The second one was doing a lot of drugs to keep her weight down. The youngest had just gone off with a German man when they discovered she was pregnant.

This passage, an indirect internal monologue by Yolanda's lover Clive, offers an outsider's succinct summary of the dynamics of the García family. Yolanda's mother happens to sit next to Clive at a poetry reading and begins telling him about Yolanda's childhood, unaware that he is her daughter's lover. Although Clive is vague on the details, he captures the gist of each girl's narrative, hitting on the psychiatry that unites Carla and her husband, Sandra's unhealthy obsession with weight loss and appearance, and Sofía's central act of rebellion. His wry, somewhat amused tone suggests both respect for the girls' adventurous spirits and pity for what he perceives to be their troubled, unsettled tendencies. Such a brief outline of each daughter's life would lead a casual observer to conclude that the family is wildly dysfunctional. The novel, however, paints a more complex picture by focusing on the overpowering family devotion that binds the Garcías together despite their intense, divergent convictions.

"The others aren't bad looking, don't get me wrong. But Sandi, Sandi got the fine looks, blue eyes, peaches and ice cream skin, everything going for her!" The mother spread her arms in all directions to show how pretty and pale and blue-eyed the girl was. Bits of her Kleenex fell to the floor, and she picked off the specks from the carpet. "My great-grandfather married a Swedish girl, you know? So the family has light-colored blood, and that Sandi got it all. But imagine, spirit of contradiction,

she wanted to be darker complected like her sisters."

How the GarcÃ–a Girls Lost Their Accents, pg. 52

Sandra has recently been committed to a private mental hospital for an eating disorder and nervous breakdown during graduate school. Laura describes Sandra to the doctor, emphasizing her pale, blue-eyed appearance as her most important distinguishing characteristic. This episode is the novel's first lengthy discussion of Sandra. However, later chapters reveal Sandra as a complex and conflicted person obsessed with the dynamics of social power. She recognizes that her beauty gives her influence, but she becomes a manic dieter and is never satisfied with herself. She is both the most beautiful and the least happy sister, but Laura fails to understand the connection between the two poles. To Laura, stuck in the traditional Dominican value system that privileges fair good looks, Sandra's appearance has a straightforward advantage: it will help her find a husband. Laura's uncontrolled, dramatic gestures indicate her bafflement at Sandra's condition. She sees the woman's role as being attractive, finding a husband, and keeping house, a model that leaves no room for an ambitious, beautiful daughter who would prefer to be ugly. From this passage, the reader begins to realize that Laura's inability to understand or sympathize with Sandra's state of mind has probably exacerbated her daughter's illness.

Our next workshop, no one understood what my sublimated love sonnet was all about, but Rudy's brought down the house. Suddenly, it seemed to me, not only that the world was full of English majors, but of people with a lot more experience than I had. For the hundredth time, I cursed my immigrant origins. If only I too had been born in Connecticut or Virginia, I too would understand the jokes everyone was making on the last two digits of the year, 1969; I too would be having sex and smoking dope; I too would have suntanned parents who took me skiing in Colorado over Christmas break, and I would say things like "no shit," without feeling like I was imitating someone else.

How the GarcÃ–a Girls Lost Their Accents, pgs. 94-5

During her first year at a co-ed college, Yolanda begins to discover how her immigrant upbringing has affected not only her relation to English and language, but to sexuality as well. The Americans around her seem more comfortable in their skin, just as they are more comfortable with the language. Yolanda, meanwhile, cannot use English casually, nor can she shed her belief in the sanctity of sex. In this chapter, Yolanda tries to understand why she refused Rudy's persistent requests to sleep with her and took such offense at the crude slang he used to describe sex. This interior monologue clarifies the relation Yolanda perceives between linguistic vernacular, a sense of belonging or acceptance, and an uninhibited attitude towards sex.

We don't even try anymore to raise consciousness here. It'd be like trying for cathedral ceilings in a tunnel, or something. Once, we did take on Tía Flor, who indicated her large house, the well-kept grounds, the stone Cupid who had been re-routed so it was his mouth that spouted water. "Look at me, I'm a queen," she argued. "My husband has to go to work every day, I can sleep until noon, if I want. I'm going to protest for my rights?"

How the GarcÃ–a Girls Lost Their Accents, pg. 121

Having adjusted to American teenage life, the García sisters are increasingly disturbed by the misogynist culture that even women in the Dominican Republic embrace. Here, the three older sisters are visiting Sofía during her year in the Dominican Republic, and commenting on the atmosphere of political indifference among Dominican women. The chapter is written in the first person plural ("we") so that the three sisters seem to act as a coalition, unified against the culture they fear is sapping Sofía's independent spirit. The passage hints at how different the sisters' worldview might have been had they remained on the Island and grown up as privileged, pampered women in an unquestioning patriarchy. The metaphor of Dominican culture as a tunnel reflects the narrow blindness with which the sisters see Dominican women obeying and supporting the patriarchy. The concept of "rights," of which Tía Flor is so incredulous, becomes a temple of enlightenment and freedom compared to the closed darkness of Dominican culture. Additionally, the euphemistic detail of the Cupid who has been "re-routed" suggests the girls' amusement at the sanitized attitude older Dominican women take towards sex.

As usual, we're to wait for the lovers at Capri's. Twenty minutes before our curfew, they'll pick up Carla, and we'll all head home again like one big happy group of virgin cousins. But tonight, as we've agreed, we're staging a coup on the same Avenida where a decade ago the dictator was cornered and wounded on his way to a tryst with his mistress. It was a plot our father helped devise but did not carry through, since by then we had fled to the States. Tonight, we are blowing the lovers' cover. First step is to get Mundín to drive us home. Male loyalty is what keeps the macho system going, so Mundín will want to protect Manuel.

How the GarcÃ–a Girls Lost Their Accents, pg. 127

This passage makes one of the few explicit comments on the parallel between the Dominican family patriarchy and Trujillo's dictatorship. The three elder sisters have concocted a scheme to separate the teenage Sofía from her cousin, Manuel Gustavo, whom she has been dating while living in the Dominican Republic. Earlier in the chapter, the sisters compare Manuel's domineering behavior to tyranny, implying that Trujillo's dictatorship gains some of its staying power from the patriarchal culture the expects masculine dominance and demands unquestioning submission from women. Trujillo fulfills the traditional model of a macho man, but Manuel's pettiness and ignorance indicate how superficial and uninspiring that masculine archetype is when viewed critically. One of the novel's ironies is that the girls'

Quotes and Analysis

father, who risked his life to oust Trujillo, nevertheless unwittingly perpetrates a private form of patriarchal despotism over his wife and daughters. As outsiders to the masculine structure and to Dominican culture, the four girls are among the few who can clearly and critically analyze the "macho system."

"By all means, wait for him, but please not under this hot sun." Laura switches into her grand manner. The grand manner will usually disarm these poor lackeys from the countryside, who have joined the SIM, most of them, in order to put money in their pockets, food and rum in their stomachs, and guns at their hips. But deep down, they are still boys in rags bringing down coconuts for el patrón when he visits his fincas with his family on Sundays

How the GarcÃ−a Girls Lost Their Accents, pgs. 201-2

Laura relies on her high social status to intimidate the two thugs from the secret police (SIM) who have come to the house to interrogate Carlos. Her assumptions about their backgrounds turn out to be accurate, as an internal monologue by one of the thugs, Pupo, reveals. The machismo of the SIM agents, who want to enjoy creature comforts while exerting power through intimidation, is defined largely by the sexualized violence suggested by their guns. However, Laura believes that they adopt this swaggering attitude to cover their ingrained subservience to members of the upper classes. The passage comments on the rigid social hierarchy that allows little social mobility and is reinforced by class-based stigmas. The caste system relies so heavily on a culture of obedience that even semi-trained government agents, when encountering signals of high social rank, will revert to the behavior of their social class of birth.

It seemed with so much protocol, I would never get to draw the brilliant and lush and wild world brimming over inside me. I tried to keep my mind on the demonstration, but something began to paw the inside of my drawing arm. It clawed at the doors of my will, and I had to let it out. I took my soaking brush in hand, stroked my gold cake, and a cat streaked out on my paper in one lightning stroke, whiskers, tail, meow and all!

I breathed a little easier, having gained a cat-sized space inside myself. Doña Charito's back was to me. The hummingbird on her Hawaiian shift plunged its swordlike beak between the mounds of her bottom. There would be time.

How the GarcÃ−a Girls Lost Their Accents, pg. 247

In this passage from her girlhood in the Dominican Republic, Sandra describes her compulsion to draw and her frustration with Doña Charito's lectures during her first art lesson. Like Yolanda's nervous, creative energy, which she imagines as a bird flapping free of her chest, Sandra's urgent desire to draw or paint takes the form of an animal that clamors for freedom. This metaphor compares creativity to an untamed, animalistic impulse that Sandra can set free by drawing. Sandra's sensuous, lively visions align with the Dominican attitude towards art, which the servants and even her family members view superstitiously. A servant, Milagros, believes a drawing of her baby has the power to afflict him with fever, and the family wonders if erasing Sandra's cats from a stucco wall has brought a rat infestation. This notion of art as living and active conflicts with the formal, academic studies Doña Charito wants to impose on her pupils. Sandra's innate childhood creativity is unfortunately delicate and is stamped out of her by months of isolation and pampering after she breaks her arm.

Then we moved to the United States. The cat disappeared altogether. I saw snow. I solved the riddle of an outdoors made mostly of concrete in New York. My grandmother grew so old she could not remember who she was. I went away to school. I read books. You understand I am collapsing all time now so that it fits in what's left in the hollow of my story? I began to write, the story of Pila, the story of my grandmother. I never saw Schwarz again. The man with the goatee and Kashtanka vanished from the face of creation. I grew up, a curious woman, a woman of story ghosts and story devils, a woman prone to bad dreams and bad insomnia. There are still times I wake up at three o'clock in the morning and peer into the darkness. At that hour and in that loneliness, I hear her, a black furred thing lurking in the corners of my life, her magenta mouth opening, wailing over some violation that lies at the center of my art.

How the GarcÃ-a Girls Lost Their Accents, pgs. 289-90

In this strange paragraph that closes the novel, Yolanda muses on the relation between real life and storytelling by exploring the subtle, unexpected ways that a seemingly trivial event in her childhood has influenced her life over the years. When she was a young girl, she stole and then abandoned a kitten called Schwarz, and was haunted by visions of the mother cat for months. The accumulated effect of these visions was anxiety, insomnia and the excitement of an already active imagination. Although young Yolanda could not articulate her feelings fully, she later came to identify the sinister vision of the cat with guilt and fear. Throughout the novel, Yolanda explains that she tells stories to understand how past events came about and have shaped her present self. The black cat thus becomes a symbol of unresolved emotions that compel her to write (to practice her art) in order to tame and understand them. The cat can be a violent, wild, and uncontrollable animal, and so suggests a fierce, irrational, and wordless energy that she must struggle to put into words and fit into a pattern in her life, and thereby subdue. The potency of the final image, however, hints that the cat can never be fully tamed, and will always lurk in corners of her unconscious where her rational mind cannot reach.

Summary and Analysis of "Antojos"

This chapter, focused on Yolanda, tells of her arrival in the Dominican Republic from the United States. She has not been back to the Island in five years and is greeted with excitement by her aunts and cousins at Tía Carmen's house. The aunts recount recent stories and complain that the hired help is increasingly unreliable. Yolanda updates them about her sisters, and she is prompted to speak in Spanish when she slips into English. She thinks to herself that she may not return to the United States, but keeps this thought a secret.

Tía Carmen asks if she has any little antojo, an old Spanish word referring to a whim or craving that seizes someone when he is taken over by a santo (saint). Yolanda does not recognize the word, so the aunts call on an elderly servant, Altagracia, to explain. Yolanda says she craves freshly picked guavas, and suggests she might pick some when she goes north in a few days. The family disputes the safety of her plan to drive a car into the interior given the political situation, and decide a Datsun will attract less attention than a Volvo. They discuss the possibility of guerillas in the mountains, while a private guard walks by their own compound. Then they light the candles on Yolanda's welcome cake and, as she bends to blow them out, Yolanda wishes that the Island would remain her home.

The second half of the chapter follows Yolanda on her trip north to Altamira, where she is visiting the estate of her wealthy relatives the Mirandas. On the way, she stops at a cantina run by an old woman and her young son, José Duarte, Sánchez y Mella, named after the country's three liberators. José and his friends offer to bring Yolanda guavas, but she wants to pick them herself, so she drives the boys to the guava grove. There, Yolanda and José wander away to pick fruit, and it grows late as they find their way back. Her aunt's warnings about the dangers of the interior begin to grow in Yolanda's mind, intensifying when she discovers that her car has a flat tire.

While José runs to the Miranda mansion for help, Yolanda sees two laborers emerge onto the road with machetes hanging from their belts. Terrified and seemingly paralyzed, Yolanda is unable to answer their questions. Then, one suggests she is American and speaks no Spanish. Yolanda bursts into a stream of rapid English, of which the men only understand the name "Miranda." It is not clear whether the men meant Yolanda any harm, but the name "Miranda" acts as a charm and they suddenly seem benign toward her. They fix her flat tire for her, refusing her offered payment until she simply stuffs the bills into one's pocket. When she drives away, she meets a crying José coming back from the Miranda house, where the guard accused the boy of lying and hit him.

Analysis

The chapter focuses on the socio-economic disparity Yolanda sees in the Dominican Republic and the ways in which her status as part of a wealthy family and as an

American-bred girl affect her relations with her family and people she encounters on the Island. To her, many Dominicans seem like prisoners trapped in their rigid social hierarchy. While visiting her wealthy relatives the Mirandas, she uses a simile to compare the guard in the enclosed estate to "a man locked in a strangely gorgeous prison" (14). The guard later hits José, not believing that a Dominican woman wealthy enough to own a car would be out picking guavas. This rigid set of expectations for how people of certain classes behave forms part of the structure that perpetuates strict division between classes.

Yolanda falls into this way of thinking as well when she meets the two laborers on the road. She assumes they mean to harm her and is petrified with fear. When they first appear, the description of them is short and clipped, with direct, simple sentences, such as "Machetes hang from their belts" (19). The terse style indicates how Yolanda, in her fright, sees the men. She notices aspects of them that suggest strength or violence and therefore indicate ways they might hurt her.

When the men mistake her for an American and hear the name of her wealthy hosts, they are described as becoming "docile" (20), as though they are wild creatures that can be tamed only by those they believe hold higher social status than themselves. They become embarrassed by their rough, dirty hands, and Yolanda observes that they assume the same pose of looking at the ground that the servant Iluminada and young José do. This shared gesture unites many members of the lower classes Yolanda has encountered, and marks how universal the mindset of obedience and hierarchy is in the country.

Yolanda, as an outsider to the country, observes this and other gestures with interest. She has not learned the cultural cues that teach her what different types of body language mean, and so sees their gestures with detachment. She compares the body language of her family and her servants to those she has seen in a book for Renaissance actors, indicating that Dominican social behavior is as distant from her own life as centuries' old acting conventions.

The most vivid indication of how strange Yolanda feels in the country, though, is her impression of the poster for Palmolive soap outside the cantina at Altamira. Yolanda recognizes that the billboard communicates nothing about soap, but conveys a cultural message instead. The sensual blond woman who seems to cry out in wordless ecstasy suggests how American culture is seen as sexualized and desirable to Dominicans. When Yolanda sees the billboard at the end of the chapter, she describes the woman as "calling someone over a great distance" (23), no longer sexy but still trying to catch someone's attention. Metaphorically, the "great distance" could be the cultural gap between the Dominican Republic and the United States, where the woman comes from. The woman is exotic to Dominicans, and her wordless cry implies a lack of true reciprocity in the cultural exchange between Dominicans and Americans. Each side holds stereotyped visions of the other, since the cultures are radically different, and use their own largely incompatible standards to judge each other. For Yolanda, the poster thus becomes a symbol of the failed cultural exchange, and of the difficulties she will have acclimating herself to the life she hopes to lead in the Dominican Republic.

Summary and Analysis of "Antojos"

Summary and Analysis of "The Kiss"

Even after the four García girls have been married or begun raising families, they still return home alone for an intimate family reunion on their father's birthday. This year, though, the youngest girl, Sofía, wants to hold the celebration at her house. She does not want to travel because of her four-year-old daughter and newborn son, but she also does not want to miss the celebration, since she is now on speaking terms with her father for the first time since she eloped with her German husband Otto six years ago. Sofía's son is the first boy born into the family in two generations, and is named Carlos after his maternal grandfather. His fair Germanic looks, name, and masculinity make him a favorite of Carlos, who coos the name of famous men named Charles over the crib, much to Sofía's disgruntlement.

Sofía is characterized as the daughter with a fiercely independent spirit and a constant string of boyfriends. She dropped out of college and worked as a secretary while dating a man with whom she thought herself in love. Unable to sleep with him in New York, she went on vacation to Bogotá, Colombia with him, but soon lost interest. While in Colombia, she met a German tourist on the streets and fell in love. Though she hid the relationship, her father was suspicious and searched her drawers until she found Otto's love letters. Furious, he demanded an explanation from Sofía and asked if she were a whore, after which she snarled a curse at him, packed her bags, and left the house. She managed to fly to Germany, found Otto's house, and asked him to marry her. She discovered only afterward that he was a world-class chemist, but even his fame did not appease her father.

When Sofía's daughter was born at her new house in Michigan, her mother flew out to visit the family, dragging Carlos in tow. However, he refused to speak with Sofía. The next year Sofía came to the house for his birthday. Though she spent the next six years slowly trying to patch up their relationship, he remained stiff and distant.

The narration jumps forward to Carlos' seventieth birthday, to be held the same day as Sofía's son's christening. A large contingent of the family would be convening in Michigan for the party, including all the daughters' husbands for the first time. Sofía planned the party with excruciating care, hiring a band, buying paper hats, pins, and balloons, and planning eating and sleeping arrangements. At first, the party goes off splendidly, with gifts, toasts, and live music. However, one paragraph of free indirect narration reveals that Carlos feels out of place and superfluous among his daughters' young, fancy, high-talking friends, comparing their youth and inexperience to his long, eventful life and imagining how little material impact his death would have on their lives.

Noticing his sour mood, Yolanda arranges a game in which Carlos sits blindfolded in a chair while his daughters peck him on the cheek or forehead; he must then guess which daughter kissed him. Sofía is in the bedroom tending to her son, but when she returns, she notices that her father never guesses her name. Upset, she decides to surprise him by slowly licking his ear in a sensuous way. Furious at having been aroused in public by his own daughter, he snatches the blindfold from his face and angrily ends both the game and the party.

Analysis

This chapter focuses on Carlos García's masculine pride of ownership and control. He writes his name on the top bill of the stacks he gives his daughters, as though claiming possession of them. By refusing to give them money when their husbands are present, he implies a connection between economic power and manhood. At his party, he becomes depressed when he realizes that his professional, educated daughters and his resourceful wife do not depend on him as women are expected to in Dominican culture. He does not imagine the emotional role he could play in their life, nor does he admit that his insistence on patriarchal values has excluded him from large parts of his daughters' lives.

The chapter hints at the superficiality of a patriarchal system based on gender roles and family status determined by birth. Ironically, the Germanic male child that will provide "good blood" to the family lineage is born to the most rebellious daughter, and from a marriage never approved by her parents. Nevertheless, Carlos dotes on the child that will keep his name alive in the United States.

However, the girls remain loving daughters who, despite their progressive feminism, have "devotions...like roots" that are "sunk into the past towards the old man" (24). Their family ties, like an invisible or hidden part of themselves, keep them attached to their father despite their American values of independence and female equality. Beneath the superficial structure of patriarchal power, these loving family bonds, like tree roots, bring the true nourishment of affection to the family.

Even Sofía feels the pull of these deep roots, although she has one of the most forceful personalities in the novel. The chapter contains various similes comparing Sofía to a natural force such as a "powerful, tamed animal" (28) or calling her face as impassive as a "pale ivory moon" (30) that pulls the tide of her father's anger when he finds her love letters. These comparisons suggest how Sofía's instinctive confidence and comfort in her own skin give her an aura of strength that even her father's fury cannot overcome. Also like a force of nature, she follows her own principles and does not strive to conform to either American or Dominican expectation. She rejects the American ideal of personal ambition, dropping out of college and abandoning pursuit of a career. She also refuses to obey the edicts of the Dominican patriarchy. Perhaps because she does not accept outwardly imposed rules, she acts and speaks without artificiality or nervous self-doubt.

The kiss Sofía gives her father at the end of the party is an example of how she refuses to play by the rules. She makes a statement with her kiss, rather than simply offering the daughterly kisses given by everyone else. The kiss is the emotional climax of the scene, and the chapter builds up to it by repeatedly mention that

Summary and Analysis of "The Kiss"

everyone has drunk too much. Although there is no warning that something might go wrong, the repetition of the statement that the guests are all drunk hints that the party is beginning to spin out of control and so create a tense, expectant mood for the reader. Ironically, Sofía is one of the few characters not drunk, since she has been too busy throughout the party. Instead, it is her bold personality and refusal to play things safe that causes problems.

Summary and Analysis of "The Four Girls"

This chapter opens when Sofía (the youngest daughter) is twenty-six and the Carla (the oldest) almost thirty-one years old. It begins by discussing how their mother handled raising four girls so close in age. Their mother has always called them "the four girls" or used a general pet name, "Cuquita," as far back as they can remember. When they were young, their mother color-coded their clothing and belongings to prevent confusion and jealousy among them. Carla, who became a child psychologist, later wrote an autobiographical essay, "I Was There Too," arguing that the color-coding had weakened the girls' identity differentiation abilities.

Their mother identifies each girl with a favorite story she likes to tell about that daughter. She begins with a story about Carla as a young child, when the family was still quite poor. Carla wanted a pair of red sneakers, but the family could not afford any unnecessary expense. One day a neighbor received a pair of sneakers as a gift for her daughter, but the shoes did not fit. Knowing how relentlessly Carla had been pestering her mother for sneakers, the neighbor offered the shoes to the Garcías. However, Carla demanded that the shoes be red, and refused to wear them until her father secretly painted them with his wife's nail polish.

The next story shifts to Yolanda, the third eldest girl, who holds a graduate degree and writes poetry. Her mother believed she would be "the famous one," but Yolanda has become a literature teacher, not a poet. She still gives readings, though, which her mother attends, seemingly unfazed by the explicit sexual content of many of Yolanda's poems. At one reading, Yolanda's mother unknowingly sits next to Yolanda's lover, Clive, who is the head of the Comparative Literature department where Yolanda teaches. Clive pretends not to know Yolanda, and listens to her mother tell the story of a trip the family took to New York when Yolanda was three years old. Yolanda had been accidentally left aboard a New York bus, and when her parents finally caught up with the bus after running frantically for two blocks, they found her reciting Edgar Allan Poe's "Annabel Lee" to a crowd of people.

The narrator next explains that Laura García no longer tells her favorite story about Sandra, excusing herself by saying she would like to forget the past. Sandra was recently committed to a private mental hospital called Mount Hope, where her mother told the senior psychiatrist, Dr. Tandlemann, about the beginning of Sandra's anorexia and nervous breakdown. Dr. Tandlemann corrects Laura whenever she calls her daughter "crazy," but he soon realizes that Sandra's condition extends beyond her eating disorder. Sandra, who inherited the fair skin and blue eyes of a distant Swedish ancestor, became devoted to her good looks and began going on dangerous crash diets. While in graduate school, she was hospitalized. When her parents arrived at the hospital, they found her reading frantically. She explained that she needed to read as many books as possible before she turned into a monkey, and she refused to eat meat, arguing that she might become a chicken or red snapper, since evolution had reached its peak and was now reversing. As Laura tells Dr. Tandlemann the story, Carlos, who has been looking out the window, sees Sandra walking across the lawn with a nurse. Without seeing her father, Sandra suddenly breaks into panicked run, having mistaken the lawnmower as a roaring animal on a leash

The final story also takes place at a hospital, but this time at the birth of Sofía's daughter, Laura's first granddaughter. As Laura admires the newborn, she strikes up a conversation with a young man whose wife has just given birth. Laura begins to tell the man about Sofía, who she says has always been a smart and lucky girl. She relates how the García house was burgled on the night Sofía was born, but the police caught the men and returned the stolen items. Then she erroneously tells him how Sofía met her German husband Otto on a church trip to Perú (Sofía actually met him when she followed her then-boyfriend to Colombia).

In the next scene, a week after the birth of Sofía's daughter, the four sisters are gathered together for Christmas. It is early morning and the sisters are exchanging news before the other family members awake. Each girl is under emotional stress, and their intimate conversation is occasionally interrupted by bickering. Sandra has been released from Mount Hope psychiatric hospital a month ago, and Yolanda's lover, Clive, has just gone back to his wife. The sisters unite, though, in laughing over their mother's inaccurate story of Sofía's marriage, from which she omits unsavory elements such as how Sofía ran away and eloped. The sisters begin to mimic playfully their father's violent reaction to the love letters he had found, although Sofía reminds them that her father still refuses to speak with her. Soon after, Laura, Carlos, Otto, and Carla's husband join them in the living room and Laura begins to relate a recent dream she had about the baby.

Analysis

Each story Laura tells about her daughters captures a unique moment in that girl's life, and expresses some particular idiosyncrasy or personality trait of that daughter. At the same time, they create a shared history that binds the family together. Storytelling also reveals much about the teller and the audience. Examining how or why people tell or listen to stories offers clues about their attitudes towards the story's subject and each other.

The stories Laura tells in this chapter do not relate formative moments. Instead, they either discuss minor incidents in the girls' childhoods or, in Sandra's case, describe a later event with an unknown cause. The story of Carla's red sneakers, for instance, tells of a trivial but memorable incident. It immerses its audience in a specific moment of the family's past—when Laura and Carlos were recently married and still poor—and establishes the family's internal dynamics.

The way the listeners react to the story in the outer frame narrative offers considerable insight into their characters. Carla emphasizes the color red in the story, indicating that she is searching for hidden sexual meanings in the story. Her interpretation of the story reveals more about her thought patterns than about the story itself, and demonstrates how focusing narrowly on one aspect of a story can distort it. Meanwhile, Carla's husband rubs Carla's back in sensual circles and fondles her shoulder "as if it were a breast" (45), a simile that suggests that Carla's entire body is sexualized for her husband. This description of their interaction presents a reductive and incomplete view of the couple as obsessed with sex. While there is no question that they are preoccupied with sexual behavior, the narrator has exaggerated that aspect of them to the exclusion of other traits. This tendency highlights the fundamental difference between real life and stories: the process of selection. By selecting which details to include, the storyteller gains the advantage of establishing patterns that might not otherwise be visible, but they also sacrifice completeness in their vision of the subject.

Similarly, the way Laura tells Dr. Tandlemann about Sandra's mental breakdown reveals attitudes Laura holds that might have contributed to Sandra's problems. When describing Sandra, Laura emphasizes her pale skin and blue eyes as her distinguishing characteristics, not mentioning the complex emotional and mental life Sandra demonstrates in other chapters. Sandra is both the most beautiful and the least happy sister, but Laura fails to understand the connection between the two poles. To Laura, stuck in the traditional Dominican value system that privileges fair good looks, Sandra's appearance has a straightforward advantage: it will help her find a husband. Laura's failure to understand or sympathize with Sandra's state of mind has probably exacerbated her daughter's illness.

In the chapter's final scene, the daughters gather and tell stories about their parents. Aspects of their lives that were showcased in the four previous stories—Carla's psychology jargon, Yolanda's poetry and her lover Clive, Sandra's breakdown and Sofía's daughter—all come into play. Sofía comments that there is "Nothing like a story to take the sting out of things" (65), pointing out anther value to storytelling as a way of understanding and coming to terms with difficult situations. These various observations about storytelling inform the rest of the novel, which is similarly structured as a series of tales.

Summary and Analysis of "Joe"

The chapter opens by explaining that the title, "Joe," is the English mispronunciation of Yolanda's nickname "Yo." Yolanda stands at a window watching a man she calls "Doc" walk across the lawn with a tennis ball and racket. She imagines him as the son of tycoons and begins playing with the word "tycoon" and the names of objects in the room. Unseen, she blows him a kiss. She is apparently in love with him, but her language is so random and disorienting that the course of her thoughts seems unstructured and illogical.

Yo begins narrating her own memories to herself, as if she were talking to Doc. She explains that she loved John at first, and then flashes back to different scenes and dialogues that occurred between her and John, now her ex-husband. Her language is strangely poetic and surreal, and the two lovers jokingly speak in rhyme, although Yolanda has a more poetic ear for the sound of language than John does.

The scene shifts abruptly to an argument in which John tells Yolanda to see a shrink. She feels uncomfortable with his crude slang and idiomatic expressions like "shrink" and "push comes to shove," and she begins to feel that she cannot trust him. Yolanda lists John's fastidious behaviors, such as folding his clothes after lovemaking, and concludes that John is too much a realist to live in her poetical world with her. In particular, she reminisces about finding John's list weighing the pros and cons of marrying her. She found the list after she had started seeing a psychiatrist, Doctor Payne (Doc), and confronted John about whether he had to decide he loved her or not.

In the next scene, John tries to kiss and make love to Yolanda, who resists angrily. There follows a scene, which probably occurs soon after, in which John brings home blue flowers for Yolanda. Yolanda recognizes kindness in John's tone, but, bizarrely, cannot understand his words. She hears only "babble, babble" and John reveals that he cannot understand her either, leading Yolanda to hope that they have exhausted language and can return to silence.

Yolanda writes a note to John and returns to her parents, who become concerned by her habit of ceaselessly talking in quotations. She quotes poets like Frost, Stevens, Rilke and Rumi, and even sings children's rhymes throughout dinner and during her sessions with Doctor Payne. The doctor decides to check her into a small, private facility where he can keep an eye on her. During her treatment, she finds herself falling in love with Doc. She also develops what she calls an "allergic reaction" to certain words, so that saying "love" or "alive" causes her eyes to water and skin to itch.

Finally, the narrative returns to the opening scene in which Yolanda is watching Doc with his tennis gear. She imagines a beating hunger—heartbreak—inside her that emerges like a dark bird and swoops down on Doc, who is sunning on the lawn. His red towel turns into a pool of blood for Yolanda, who cries out to him. He tries to guess who is calling his name from the window until Yolanda shouts her name at him. The name causes her to feel uncomfortably itchy, the signs of her allergic reaction to words, and she ends the chapter by saying various words aloud to test how she will react to them.

Analysis

Yolanda's psychological instability emerges from her hypersensitivity to sex and language, which she cannot separate from each other. The dangerous aspect of Yolanda's obsession with language is the temptation to build alternate worlds that she is either unwilling or unable to distinguish from the Real World, as she calls it. As she speaks with John, his words "throw themselves off the tip of his tongue like suicides" (73) or she swallows her words and feels them "beat against her stomach" (75) violently. Words have a dramatic physical existence for her and can spin fantastic visions of beasts howling in a river. When she watches the "black bird" (83) of her broken heart attack Doc, she is startled into thinking the bird might actually hurt him. Her perception itself becomes distorted, and she briefly mistakes Doc's red towel for blood. Her inner world is so vivid that it overwhelms the Real World.

Yolanda takes an ironic tone in capitalizing "Real World" (73), implying that she considers it to be an idea just like her own internal world; the Real World has been legitimized only because enough people believe in it. She says nothing explicit on the subject, but her tone of alienation from the Real World points again to the danger of her preoccupation with language. If the Real World only has significance through the symbolic order of language, there is nothing to prevent her from creating her own equally legitimate Personal World. She even invokes the creative power of God's Word when alludes to the opening of the Bible, "In the beginning" (70). She resists placing limits on words' power to create.

John, however, is a firm believer in the Real World. He is methodical and unimaginative and speaks in clichés that indicate his relative indifference to language. By the end of their marriage, the difference in their respective interest in language has been amplified until it seems to Yolanda that they do not speak the same language at all. When John brings her flowers to reconcile with her, she hears only "babble babble" (78). John is speaking English, but his words meaning nothing to her and metaphorically become nonsense syllables.

When she leaves John, she begins to speak only in quotations of other writers, as though she finds language so overwhelmingly powerful that she fears to use her own words. As her therapy with Doc progresses, he urges her to use only her own words, forcing her to confront the meanings of what she says. She becomes frustrated at her inability to define crucial abstractions like "love" or "Yolanda" accurately, and she develops allergic reactions, such as itchy skin and watery eyes, to saying these words. Such words mean too much and nothing at all, whereas Yolanda wants a precise correspondence between the word and what it signifies.

Doc tries to teach her that not every emotion or idea needs to be articulated in language. Some experiences, he suggests, exist outside the symbolic order of language, and are real despite being indefinable.

Summary and Analysis of "The Rudy Elmenhurst Story"

Yolanda opens by explaining that she and her sisters have a tradition of telling each other stories at night to determine who was the "wildest." For a while, at boarding school, Yolanda's "vivacious" personality attracted many callers. When she reached college, though, she found that most of her relationships did not last because she refused to sleep with her admirers. Her Catholicism had lapsed, as had her "Old World" background, yet for some reason she felt uncomfortable about sex. She explains that she is telling this story in order to work out why she never slept with Rudy Elmenhurst.

Yolanda describes one of her first English classes, in which she came over-prepared and felt out of place; she refers to feeling like an "immigrant" or "greenhorn." This feeling is linked to her lack of social experience, her awkwardness with the English language and her family's idiosyncrasies. Rudolf Brodermann Elmenhurst, the third, is the only student absent from the class, and she feels a connection with this unknown person because he, too, seems an outsider. When he breezes in ten minutes late to class, completely unprepared, it turns out he is very comfortable in most social situations and experiences none of Yolanda's acute discomfort. She is too embarrassed to ask that he return a pencil she lends him, and flees the classroom right after class. At 10:30 that night, he knocks on her door, offering the pencil back. She has been working on the love sonnet assigned for the English class, and tells him she's doing homework. She does not trust Rudy, feeling that she "had nothing in my vocabulary of human behavior to explain him" (92). However, she agrees to have lunch with him the next day. At lunch, they talk nonstop until dinner, and are soon dating.

Despite his insistent coaxing, however, she refuses to have sex with him. She helps him write his love sonnet for English, and is surprised to discover in class that all of the images have hidden sexual meanings. She is so ignorant, in fact, that Rudy has to draw diagrams of her reproductive organs to explain why she will not necessarily get pregnant if she sleeps with him. Ultimately, however, she is troubled by Rudy's careless attitude towards language, sex, and even other symbols like the American flag. She wants sex to be elevated, as she believes language should be. After he insults her about her unwillingness to sleep with him, she leaves his bedroom and holds herself aloof for the next few weeks. She fantasizes and dreams about him helplessly, but makes no moves. Finally, at the spring dance, she sees him with another girl and realizes this girl has been the beloved of all his poems for their English class.

Yolanda resumes the story five years later while in graduate school in upstate New York. She has become bohemian, taken lovers, dropped acid, and is on birth control. One night she receives a call from Rudy asking to come over. He brings a fancy bottle of wine, but again his crude, casual attitude towards sex infuriates her and she throws him out.

Analysis

Throughout this chapter, Yolanda relies on language to guide her personal and moral choices. The story is an attempt to tease out her troubled relationship with Rudy Elmenhurst and with language. She hopes that putting the events into words will help clarify her own decisions. Ultimately, she concludes that she refused to sleep with Rudy because she saw his irreverence for language and sex as implying lack of respect for herself.

Rudy and Yolanda speak different languages, literally and figuratively. Rudy's native English and his personality give him a freewheeling attitude that Yolanda lacks. She senses that the Americans around her seem more comfortable in their skin, just as they are more comfortable with the language. Yolanda, meanwhile, cannot use English casually, nor can she shed her belief in the sanctity of sex. She is troubled by the crude terms Rudy uses for sex and by his irreverence for symbols she respects, such as using the American flag as a coverlet.

Yolanda metaphorically compares Rudy's physical gestures to a language and complains that Rudy fails to understand the importance of suggestion, connotation, and varied vocabulary in bed. Though his body is instinctively sexual, he does not see how two types of kisses may be as different from each other as "screwing" is from "making love." His failure to appreciate the subtler aspects of language is ironic given that the two have poetry class together, where they interpret texts in which every word choice can alter the meaning.

Yolanda, meanwhile, is deeply sensitive to the world of symbols. She respects symbols, including language, signs of national pride such as the flag, and of religious belief such as her crucifix. She sees continuity between the world of symbols and the physical world, sensing that one's attitude toward a symbol reflects and influences one's attitude toward the thing itself. Speaking about sex casually therefore amounts to treating sex casually—and by extension, lacking consideration for herself.

Yolanda's trouble with sexual liberty and language is also linked to her confusion about her mixed identity. Her parents are stiffer and more conservative than her American classmates' parents are, and she has not grown up with the typical crude jokes or slang that offer the first step to being at ease with one's body and sexuality. Yolanda recognizes that one's way of talking about something can influence one's attitude towards it, and her discomfort with English—revealed in her overly grammatical speech and her feeling that she's "imitating someone else" (95) when she uses coarse language—affects her feelings about sex.

By the end of the chapter, Yolanda has become sexually active, yet still refuses to sleep with Rudy. After Rudy leaves, Yolanda struggles to uncork the wine he brought, an action that may be read as an allegory for releasing her sexuality. Yet she still takes an ironic tone when she compares herself to a "decadent wild woman" (103), remaining self-conscious and distanced from her body. She recognizes that drinking from the bottle suggests oral sex, and uses her imagination to take power over an otherwise embarrassing and upsetting scene.

Summary and Analysis of "A Regular Revolution"

The chapter begins with Carlos deciding to remain in the United States when the girls are still young, due to political instability on the Island. The girls feel out of place in America, where they have only second-hand clothing and are taunted in school. When they are sent to a fancy prep school, they still feel isolated, but they begin to gain freedom from their overbearing parents. Noticing this new trend, their parents determine to send the girls back to the Dominican Republic for the summers to reconnect with their roots and to nurture a more feminine, traditional, and Catholic attitude in them.

One such summer, while they on the Island, Laura finds a baggy of marijuana Sofía had brought to the house. Sofía takes the blame for the weed, and she is given the choice of staying on the Island the following year or returning to live at home and attend a local Catholic school. She chooses to stay on the Island, where she begins to date an illegitimate cousin, Manuel Gustavo. When the other girls return to visit the following summer, they discover that she has begun wearing makeup, doing her hair, and, worst of all, obeying Manuel Gustavo's tyrannical commands about what she can wear, whom she can speak to, and so on.

On learning that the couple is having sex without contraceptives (Manuel Gustavo will not wear a condom because he thinks it causes infertility), the three girls and their cousin Lucinda scheme to break the couple up. One day, instead of waiting to pick the couple up after their night out alone, the girls convince their chaperone, their cousin Mundín, to drive them all back to the house without Sofía and Manuel Gustavo. When the girls' aunts discover that the two are alone together, they lament Sofía's tarnished reputation and Laura decides Sofía must return to the States where she can be under close supervision. When Sofía returns later that night, she denounces her sisters as traitors.

Analysis

The theme of "revolution" runs through this chapter, beginning with the political unrest that drives Carlos to settle permanently in the United States. The United States becomes a haven for revolutionaries of all sorts: just as the family fled to the States for freedom from oppression, so the girls escape the tyranny of a patriarchal family by embracing the American sexual revolution of the 1960s and 70s. While visiting the Dominican Republic, the three older sisters wage a revolution against the system of machismo that threatens to devour Sofía.

The chapter is written in the first person plural ("we"), and each girl is referred to in third person, so the three older sisters appear to act as a coalition, unified against the culture they fear is sapping Sofía's independent spirit. In their battle against the rigid gender roles of Dominican culture, they identify with Victorian feminists like Mary

Wollstonecraft, Virginia Woolf, and Susan B. Anthony. The sexual hypocrisy that these famous activists encountered in their own society closely resembles the problems the García sisters see in Dominican culture. Mundín, for instance, demonstrates a gross sexual double standard when grows angry at the suggestion that his sister is not a virgin, but applauds Manuel Gustavo's sexual activity. Similarly, many upper-class men frequent brothels like Motel Los Encantos, which has private garages so the clients cannot identify each other by their cars. As in Victorian England, Dominican society ignores the infidelity of its men, while expecting its women to remain chaste.

On the night that they "betray" Sofía and Manuel Gustavo, the sisters recognize that they are on the same avenue where Trujillo was attacked on his way to his mistress. Their father had helped devise this coup, but had fled to the United States by the time it was carried out. The girls' revolution against corrupt male rule and despotic sexual hypocrisy thus parallels the revolutionary attempt to overthrow a corrupt dictatorship. Throughout the chapter, the three sisters compare Manuel Gustavo's domineering behavior to "tyranny," implying congruence between political and private patriarchy. The metaphor suggests that Trujillo derives power from the underlying patriarchal culture that expects masculine dominance and demands unquestioning submission from the female half of the population.

Trujillo fulfills the traditional model of a macho man, but Manuel's pettiness and ignorance indicate how superficial and uninspiring that masculine archetype is when viewed critically. The sisters nickname Manuel Gustavo "M.G.," a type of car they associate with sleazy, macho Dominican men, and they "rev up" by crying "Rrrmm, rrrmm" whenever they hear a misogynist comment. "Revving up" becomes a metonymic figure for the entire superficial, unfair system. It implies the male desire to possess the car's physical power, while hinting at the vanity and superficiality of the macho model. Machismo reduces men to cars: unthinking, flashy, and mindlessly violent.

As outsiders to the masculine structure and to Dominican culture, the four girls are among the few who can critically analyze the "macho system." One of the novel's ironies is that their father, who risked his life to oust Trujillo, nevertheless perpetrates a private form of patriarchal despotism over his wife and daughters. Even the girls' aunts embrace the misogynist system, and the sisters compare raising consciousness of women's rights on the Island with "trying for cathedral ceilings in a tunnel" (121). The metaphor of Dominican culture as a tunnel reflects the narrow blindness with which the sisters see Dominican women obeying and supporting the patriarchy. The concept of "rights" becomes a temple of enlightenment and freedom compared to the closed darkness of Dominican culture.

Summary and Analysis of "Daughter of Invention"

This chapter begins by describing Laura García's attempts at inventing improved household devices when the family first moved to New York. She would take the four girls to department stores and listen to lengthy sales pitches for household conveniences, then go home and sketch out improvements. After reading in the *New York Times* that someone has just patented a rolling suitcase, an idea she had envisioned but never acted on, she decides to stop inventing. Instead, she helps clean and keep accounts for Carlos's successful Centro de Medicina in the Bronx.

As the girls enter high school, Laura feels increasingly comfortable in the United States, while her husband begins to dream of moving back to the Dominican Republic. Trujillo's dictatorship had just been toppled and the interim government plans to hold the first free elections in thirty years. Like her mother, Yolanda has also begun to settle into America, and she explores the English language in poems and personal compositions that catch the attention of the Catholic nuns who teach at her school.

In ninth grade, she is asked to write a speech for the Teacher's Day address. Nervous at the thought of her accented English and at the teasing she will endure from her peers from praising the teachers at the assembly, Yolanda is paralyzed and cannot write. Finally, the night before the assembly, she is inspired by Walt Whitman's *Leaves of Grass* and writes an irreverent speech declaring that the best student learns to destroy the teacher. When her father hears the speech, he becomes incensed at its disrespectful message and tears it to pieces. Yolanda, in fury, accuses him of being another "Chapita," Trujillo's hated nickname. She then flees to her room and locks the door against her furious father. The locks on their bedroom doors had been her mother's idea, and for the first time Yolanda praises her mother's ingenuity.

Soon after, her mother comes to her room and helps her to write a trite speech praising the teachers, which earns Yolanda a standing ovation the following day. That night, she hides in her room when her father returns home. Eventually, as he calls up to her in apology and remorse, she comes downstairs to find that her father has bought her a fancy new typewriter tricked out with more gadgets than even her mother could have imagined. Yoyo thinks of the speech her mother helped to write as her mother's last invention, as though her mother were passing the torch of innovation and creativity onto her daughter.

Analysis

In this chapter, Laura García's inventions and Yolanda's writing mark their growing Americanization and independence from the Dominican tradition of female obedience and passivity.

The chapter's allusion to Walt Whitman highlights the American celebration of revolution and innovation that smashes the older generations' values. This cultural ideal is anathema to Dominican society, which is based on rigid hierarchies established by differences in gender and caste, and determined by birth. Laura's surname "de la Torre," for instance, received instant recognition and preferential treatment on the Island due to her family's prestige. In the United States, however, she must prove her worth on her own, and so is inspired to begin inventing and finding resourceful ways to use her energy. The loss of predetermined social status frees Laura to pursue personal growth, and Laura begins to feel that it's better to be an "independent nobody than a high-class houseslave" (144).

When Carlos asserts his adherence to the Dominican patriarchy by tearing up the Whitman-inspired speech, he becomes an oppressive authoritarian figure to Yolanda. Though the comparison of her father to "Chapita" (Trujillo) is wild exaggeration, it establishes the idea that private patriarchy is an insidious extension of political despotism. Ironically, Carlos is excited by the promise of American-style democracy in the Dominican Republic, yet cannot brook divergent viewpoints in his own family. Carlos is apparently disturbed by the suggestion that he could become, in his personal life, the very thing he opposed in the political sphere. The next day he buys Yolanda a new typewriter and explains that he only wants to protect her. This paternalistic protection, however, may be only a gentler form of the same masculine urge to control.

At the end of the chapter, Yolanda compares her mother's help writing the trite, pleasant speech she delivers to the passing on of the "pencil and pad" (149) on which Laura had invented devices. The pencil and pad becomes a metonym for female ingenuity and resourcefulness. It represents the ways that Laura, Yolanda, and all the girls rise to the challenge—and opportunity—offered by American freedom and emphasis on individual achievement.

Summary and Analysis of "Trespass"

This chapter tells the story of Carla's seventh grade year, when she attends a Sacred Heart school a few miles from home. She has only lived in the United States for a year, and her English is poor and heavily accented. At the same time that she is struggling to learn English, she must also adapt to a strange, maturing body. Since she has only begun to go through puberty, she learns the English terms for body parts and sexual organs before knowing the Spanish ones. Specifically, she learns crude playground slang that compounds the humiliation she feels about her changing body. She is teased cruelly by a gang of blond boys during recess, who shout racist and crude slurs, and molest her by pulling up her shirt.

One day, walking back from school, she is trailed by a man in a green car who stops and beckons her to the car. As she dutifully goes over to speak with him, she notices his vague, dazed look. She is shocked to discover that he is naked from the waist down and is masturbating, although she knows no words in Spanish or English to describe what he is doing. When her mother calls the police, they interview Carla about the experience, growing impatient with her inability to articulate answers to many of her questions. She imagines them as older versions of the boys on the playground, and is frightened by the threatening sexuality of their gun holsters.

Thereafter, her mother drives her to and from school. The boys stop tormenting her when they see her mother's new behavior, interpreting it as a defense against them. For the second half of seventh grade, Carla attends a public school much closer to her house.

Analysis

Carla grapples with the slippery qualities of language throughout this chapter. She strives to understand why "trespass" means different things in the Lord's Prayer and on a sign in a neighboring lot, and struggles to describe to the police the relatively simple image of a man masturbating. Although she sees the image vividly in her head, she lacks the tools to put it into communicable form, in either English or Spanish. The sexual content of the experience is no less an obstacle than her poor English. She realizes she has no word for genitalia in any language, although the policemen are able to follow her euphemistic substitutions easily enough. Her exertion reveals the immense distance that a personal experience must cross in order to be comprehended by others, a fact we often take for granted, and which the policemen do not seem to sympathize with.

The defining quality of the policemen is their indifference to her difficulties putting the image into words. Carla compares the policemen's faces to images in a movie she is watching. The metaphor suggests that the true drama is occurring in Carla's mind as she confronts the imperfect bridge that language throws over the terrifying gulf between individuals. Images on a screen, by contrast, are inhuman and require no reciprocity.

The two new realms Carla is entering—America and sexuality—are equally incomprehensible, hostile, and inescapable for her. When the boys on the playground use ugly words to describe her new body, she feels almost as if they have "the power of spells" (153) to create the body itself. Their language may not be literally magical, but it has the power of metaphor: it comes to define her body for her, rather than allowing her to come to her own private understanding of her sexual being.

Summary and Analysis of "Snow"

In this brief chapter, Yolanda recalls her first year in New York, when her family rented an apartment near a Catholic school taught by the Sisters of Charity. There, Yolanda had a grandmotherly fourth grade teacher named Sister Zoe who taught the rest of the class how to pronounce Yolanda's name. Since Yolanda was the only immigrant in the class, Sister Zoe gave her a special seat in the front row by the window, where she could tutor her in English without disturbing the rest of the class.

The Cuban Missile Crisis occurs while Yolanda is in fourth grade, and she knows enough English to understand the atmosphere of danger and fear. Sister Zoe explains the situation to the class and practices air raid drills with them. At home, Yolanda sees President Kennedy on television and says a rosary for world peace with her mother and sisters.

One morning in December, Yolanda sees white dots in the air like the radioactive dust Sister Zoe said would fall if an atomic bomb were dropped. Yolanda screams, "Bomb!" and Sister Zoe hurries to the window, then laughs and explains that the dots are flakes of falling snow. This is Yolanda's first experience of snow, and she recalls Sister Zoe telling her that each flake is different and unique, like a person.

Analysis

This chapter is narrated in the first person by Yolanda as an older woman. It reads like a personal essay written from a later vantage, with sophisticated poetic devices. In one eerie simile, she writes that the nuns who teach at the Catholic school look "like dolls in mourning" (166), a simile suggesting lifelessness and her own estrangement from their peculiar clothing and appearance. Though the women are kind to her, they are strange and unfamiliar images to her immigrant eyes, which see the world with more freshness than those that are accustomed to the United States. This initial strangeness and freshness contributes to Yolanda's active and imaginative perception, expressed in poetic images. For instance, Yolanda describes how, during her first winter, she "followed [her] breath to school" (167), imagining her breath as actively leading her. Yolanda also recalls imagining how her body would react if a bomb struck: all her hair would fall out and her arms would go soft. Her ability to place herself mentally in an alien situation is one early marker of her creativity and narrative talent.

The Cuban Missile Crisis contributes a new set of words to the popular discourse, and these enter Yolanda's vocabulary as well: terms like "nuclear bomb" and "radioactive fallout" reflect a growing anxiety about a nuclear attack. As the nation tries to define the unprecedented threats it faces, it relies on language to make comprehensible a danger it cannot totally understand. When Yolanda relates Sister Zoe's flurry of white marks on the chalkboard as the "dusty fallout that would kill us all," she adopts a subtly ironic tone that implies how futile the attempt to name, define, or depict nuclear annihilation is. After the elegance of her poetic language, she ends with three single-syllable words that declare the direct physical effect a bomb will have on her and her fellows. Those three words render all other words superfluous.

Given this omnipresent anxiety, the final simile comparing each unique crystal of snow to a person, "irreplaceable and beautiful" (167), implies both the value of each individual and the tragedy of his or her loss. The comparison reflects the threat of annihilation that plagued the dawning nuclear era, and creates an ominous mood in which the affirmation of life's beauty is undergirded by fear.

Summary and Analysis of "Floor Show"

This chapter, set three months after the family has immigrated to the States, tells the story of an outing with Dr. and Mrs. Fanning, a wealthy American couple that helped arrange Carlos's fellowship at an American hospital in order to get the family safely out of the Dominican Republic. Dr. Fanning had visited the Garcías on the Island before, to teach the country's leading doctors new procedures for heart surgery, and is now helping Carlos find a new job. Carlos cannot yet get an American doctor's license because of his foreign education, and is worried about the situation at home, where Tío Mundo is jailed and Tío Fidelio may be dead.

The Garcías' three months in New York has been made unpleasant by Carlos's worry about his family and his job at the hospital, and by "La Bruja," an elderly woman who lives below them and hurls racist slurs at the family. The Fannings have invited the García family out to El Flamenco, a fancy Spanish restaurant, where there will be a floor show of live flamenco dancing. Carlos splurges on the family, taking a taxi to the restaurant where they order drinks. Laura reminds Carlos that the Fannings are paying, causing him some discomfort.

When the Fannings arrive, Dr. Fanning suggests a job he found—a house doctor for wealthy women, unrewarding but lucrative work. As dinner continues, Sandra flirts with a handsome waiter who continually fills her water glass, until she has to use the bathroom. Her father and Mrs. Fanning go with her, and as they are about to enter their respective bathrooms, the drunk Mrs. Fanning leans in to kiss Carlos. Sandra is confused and upset by the incident, which offers a frightening glimpse of the world of sexuality she is only just starting to enter. While waiting for the adults, Sandra looks in the mirror and recognizes that she is pretty, an advantage she realizes will help her survive in this new, hostile country.

Dinner soon arrives, but Sandra finds most of the food inedible, and dedicates her time to observing the adults. Then flamenco dancing begins, and Sandra is mesmerized by the beauty and passion of the dancers, which she identifies as a Spanish quality that she too has inherited. Suddenly Mrs. Fanning runs up onstage and dances with the performers, much to the discomfort of her husband.

At the end of dinner, a salesgirl comes by with Barbies to sell. Sandra wants one that resembles the beautiful flamenco dancers onstage, and feeling vengeful towards Mrs. Fanning, loudly asserts that she wants a doll. The Fannings are happy to buy dolls for all four girls, who nevertheless receive angry glances from their mother. When asked to thank Mrs. Fanning for the doll, Sandra stands the Barbie on the table and mimes her kissing Mrs. Fanning on the cheek, saying "Gracías" so she will be true to her Spanish roots.

Analysis

Sandra is just beginning to come to terms with herself as an individual and an adult. Throughout the chapter, distinction is made between the girls' world and that of the adults, whose conversation is obscure and dull, and whose motives are inexplicable. However, Sandra observes everything keenly, including herself. She notices that she is pretty, and realizes this beauty will be her ticket to success in a new country where the Garcías are abused by prejudiced Americans. She realizes that beauty is a universal language, and personifies it as an agent that will help her, thinking, "pretty spoke both languages" (182).

The statement also reveals Sandra's awareness of the vital role language plays in social acceptance. The Garcías' bigoted neighbor, "La Bruja," had complained to the apartment building manager about the loud, foreign language the family speaks. Sandra discovers that language and good looks are both keys to social power. Another influential tool, also an underlying theme of the chapter, is money. Sandra does not realize the humiliation she causes her family by demanding the doll, which the Garcías cannot afford but are embarrassed to refuse. However, she knows that "Spanish" is validated by the fact that so many Americans are willing to pay to eat Spanish food and see Spanish entertainment at El Flamenco. Although her obsession with social status and physical appearance seems superficial, Sandra has identified the very real, inescapable power dynamics that direct social life.

In a similar situation, Carla wishes she could reject the sexuality that contributes to her isolation at school. Sandra, by contrast, embraces sexuality and her Spanish heritage as attributes that can give her power. She feels that she is entering the sexual world through her native language and heritage, and seeks a specifically Spanish sensuality. The passion of the flamenco dancers confirms her sense that sensuality inheres in Spanish culture, and that it is driven by a hidden, adult knowledge in which she wants to partake. She identifies strongly with the Barbie dressed as a flamenco dancer, which represents to her the passionate spark and hidden power of the Spanish sensuality, which she hopes she will soon possess.

Summary and Analysis of "Floor Show"

Summary and Analysis of "The Blood of the Conquistadores"

This chapter tells the story of the García family's final day on the Island. Carlos, in the kitchen, sees two thugs from the secret police approaching the house. He hides in a secret room he and Mundo built to the specifications of Victor Hubbard, a CIA agent acting as the American consul. The two men ask the García girls questions while waiting for Laura to arrive, and one makes a thinly veiled sexual suggestion to young Sofía. When Laura arrives, she sends a message with a servant using the secret code word, "tennis shoes," to bring Victor Hubbard to the house. She reminisces about Victor's plot to overthrow Trujillo, from which the U.S. State Department had withdrawn support at the last minute. Though Victor promised to get all of the men involved safely out of the country (including Carlos), Laura recalls that one conspirator, Fernando, had hung himself in his jail cell to keep from giving the others away under torture. Laura tells the men that her husband is out playing a game of tennis with Victor Hubbard, and offers them beer and snacks, putting on a "grand manner" in the hopes of disarming them.

The scene shifts to El Paraíso, a whorehouse, where the madam, Doña Tatica, receives a telephone call asking for Victor Hubbard. Hubbard, a CIA operative with a foul mouth and a pedophilic appetite for young girls, muses on his time in the Dominican Republic while he prepares to visit the García household and prevent the guardia from finding Carlos. Laura, terrified she is going to say something she shouldn't, is hugely relieved when Victor shows up. Victor announces to the men that Carlos García has received a fellowship at a hospital in the United States, and that the family's papers have received clearance from the head of Immigration, information that is new to Laura.

Briefly the perspective switches to that of Pupo, who thinks back on a warning he had heard from the man selling lottery tickets that morning, who said "The hand of God descends and some are lifted up, but some…are cast away." Pupo's recollections reveal that he and Checo had been ordered to report on Carlos' activity, but that the idea to search the house had been Checo's. Pupo suspects that the nervous Laura might be hiding something, and he anticipates uncovering a secret and earning a promotion. When Victor Hubbard arrives, however, he begins to fear that Checo's idea to search the house was a mistake for which they will both be whipped. Victor calls their supervisor, Don Fabio, and explains that Carlos will be leaving the country in forty-eight hours.

After the men leave, Laura orders her daughters to pack their best clothes and one toy they want to take to the United States. Sandra can think of no toy that means anything to her, and the narration skips ahead many years to comment that nothing—not beauty, scholarships or boyfriends—would fill the blind need which most people try to satisfy with beauty, work, food or sex.

The narration shifts to Carlos, who has been listening to his wife's high-pitched, nervous voice from the secret room over the bathroom. He worries that Laura may break down under the situation's pressure. As he listens, he thinks about his childhood as the youngest of his father's 35 children. After the men leave, Carlos is relieved to hear Laura's breathing close to him from the other side of a removable panel.

Sofía narrates the next section in first person, explaining that she was too young to remember much from their last day on the Island. However, she remembers the elderly Haitian maid, Chucha. Chucha had appeared at Papito's doorstep one night, begging for asylum after having narrowly escaped a massacre of Haitians ordered by Trujillo. While the girls are packing to leave for the States, Chucha brings a small wooden idol to them, explaining that it was the only thing she brought from Haiti when she left. She places a cup on its head filled with water that begins to evaporate and run down the statue like tears. Then she wails a prayer over each daughter, causing them to begin crying too.

The final section of this chapter is narrated by Chucha after the family has left for their flight to the States. She has been left with another servant, Chino, to tend the empty house, which she anticipates will be looted by the secret police once she dies. She predicts many tears for the family in their new country filled with people as pale as zombies. However, she also has faith in the creativity and resilience of the girls, who she thinks will adapt to their new home. After chasing bad spirits from the house, she climbs into her coffin, where she sleeps, and pulls the lid closed for a few minutes in her nightly ritual meant to prepare her for her actual burial.

Analysis

This chapter captures a wide range of Dominican voices, from the police thug Pupo, to the Haitian maid Chucha, to the madam of a brother. The reader even hears the thoughts of the pedophilic CIA agent Victor Hubbard. This narrative strategy allows the reader to see characters from other people's perspectives and so gain a fuller vision of them than an interior monologue can offer. It also emphasizes that a complete understanding of any individual is impossible.

Each person has his or her own interpretation of the dramatic events that unfold on the day the Garcías escape the SIM. By shifting rapidly between perspectives, the chapter reminds us how fragmented and multiple a single event can be. Each person receives a different impression or finds a peculiar meaning in what they observer. The young girls, for instance, misinterpret much of what the SIM men say, associating their comments with recent events in the girls' own lives. Laura and the men also have very different perceptions on their conversation before Victor arrives, while Carlos, in hiding, hears only sounds that he interprets by their tone.

Laura notes the sexual suggestion of the men's guns, implicitly linking the culture of machismo with the violence of Trujillo's military dictatorship. She relies on her high social status to intimidate the two SIM, whose backgrounds she correctly guesses to be poor and rural. The sexualized violence of their guns defines the machismo of the men, who want to enjoy creature comforts while exerting power through intimidation. However, Laura believes that they adopt a swaggering attitude to cover their ingrained subservience to members of the upper classes. The rigid Dominican class system relies so heavily on a culture of obedience that even semi-trained government agents, when encountering signals of high social rank, will revert to the behavior of the class they were born into.

The various sections are narrated in different tenses and from different vantages. Some portions of the chapter, such as Victor's section, are narrated in the present tense, creating sense of immediacy and heightened tension. Other sections are told in retrospect, either in first or third person. Sandra's section, for instance, interprets Sandra's inability to choose a favorite toy as derived from the same unsatisfied inner need that would later drive her towards a mental breakdown. Nothing she has satisfies her fully. This passage is one of the few instances in the novel in which the narrator draws an explicit connection between a childhood event and developments later in life. The purpose of reverse chronology is especially evident here, and the reader is brought to understand that the stories are told not simply to narrate the girls' lives, but to discover the underlying causes of seemingly inexplicable changes, personality traits, or decisions.

Chucha's final section, in first person and present tense, renders the events she witnesses with great immediacy. However, her way of seeing and words derived from voodoo also make parts difficult to interpret. For instance, she reports seeing loa of Carlos leave through the back door, but it is not clear whether this was Carlos himself or a vision. She interacts with spirits that no one else sees, and sees the world through the lens of her beliefs. Her section demonstrates vividly how differently a room or an object can look to two individuals.

Summary and Analysis of "The Blood of the Conquistadores"

Summary and Analysis of "The Human Body"

This chapter tells an episode from the girls' childhood on the Dominican Republic, narrated by Yolanda as an older woman. She recounts some of the trouble she got into as a young tomboy. Instead of having a female best friend, like her sisters, she liked to play with Mundín. She thinks about her grandfather, on whom Trujillo had conferred a bogus post with the United Nations. Her grandfather, whom the girls called Papito, was a peaceable man, but Trujillo felt threatened by his wealth and education, and hoped the U.N. position would keep him out of the Dominican Republic. Papito and his wife travelled to New York frequently and brought back toys for the cousins.

On one such trip, Yolanda's grandmother brings her a child's edition of the Arabian Nights, and gives Mundín a Human Body doll with removable organs, and a large ball of pink molding clay. Yolanda is jealous and asks for a swap, but Mundín refuses, so she stomps off and pretends to read her book. Unexpectedly, she finds herself engrossed in the tale of Scheherazade. In the meantime, Mundín has made a snake from his clay and is scaring the younger girl cousins until they scream and threaten to tell on him. To keep their silence, he is forced to promise them some of the clay—and promises Yolanda some as well.

Mundín demands something in return for the clay, and since he is not interested in her Arabian Nights book, he asks her to show him her private parts in exchange. To carry out the bargain, Yolanda and Mundín, with little Sofía in tow, go to the coal shed at the back of the property. This shed is supposed to be off limits to the children, since it is located near the border between Papito's property and the estate of Trujillo's daughter and son-in-law. The dictator is sometimes seen through the hedges marching across the yard with his young grandson in a little military uniform.

When both Yolanda and the uncomprehending Sofía have carried out the bargain, Mundín offers each half the clay. Yolanda throws a tantrum, demanding all the clay, and Mundín promises to give Yolanda his Human Body doll as well. However, her shouts draw the attention of the adults. Mundín's mother and the gardener find them in the shed and are about to punish them with Yolanda lies and says they were hiding in the shed from the guardia—the secret police.

The story ends with them all trooping back into the house, leaving Mundín's Human Body doll in the coal shed where he had dropped it out of fear. When they retrieve the pieces, all the organs have been chewed up or trampled and cannot be recognized or fit back together.

Analysis

In this chapter, Yolanda exhibits a growing sexual curiosity, although she remains a masculine tomboy. She unabashedly expects Mundín's Human Body doll to have genitals, and does not understand the gardener's pornographic magazine that she finds near the coal shed, although she recognizes that it was inappropriate, and that finding it has given her some power over the gardener. At the same time, she must steel herself against Mundín's gaze when she strips to show him her private parts. Mundín is similarly curious and uninterested at the same time—he is intrigued by the qualities that differentiate the sexes, but finds Yolanda's body uninteresting compared with his own.

Yolanda's only knowledge that sex is an important issue derives from adult sources. In her religious instruction classes, she has learned how original sin led Adam and Eve to feel shame at their nakedness. At home, her aunts warn her to guard her body "like hidden treasure" (235) and pressure her to stop playing with Mundín. The rigid sexual rules of Dominican society are thus imposed on her before she understands what sexuality is.

A more ominous social force, the dictatorship of Trujillo, also looms over her childhood. Her grandfather is interrogated by the SIM after Yolanda and Mundín accidentally set off a firecracker at the border of Trujillo's property, just as the dictator's grandson walks by. Yolanda lies about the guardia to escape from trouble in the coal shed, recognizing that the guardia provoke fear in her older relatives and that her own infraction will be forgotten.

At the chapter's end, Mundín and Yolanda try to put the mangled inner organs back into the Human Body doll. However, the pieces have been damaged beyond recognition and they cannot reassemble the body. The doll's destruction offers an allegory for Yolanda's maturity into knowledge of sexuality and power. Social morality, sexual rules, and the violence of the dictatorship gradually transform Yolanda from an unselfconscious child to the anxious, unsure woman she becomes. The image suggests that Yolanda was complete and unified as a child, but that her initiation into sexuality and external social systems breaks down that earlier self. When this occurs, the child becomes a "little man" (238)—a miniature version of a self-aware adult.

The process of transformation from a naïve child to an adult who experiences shame and fear parallels the Biblical story of Genesis. Yolanda alludes to the story when she thinks of her religious instruction, in which she learned that Adam and Eve had to put on clothing after they had sinned. As she begins to become ashamed of nakedness and understand the violent power behind Trujillo's dictatorship, she seems to leave her personal Eden behind.

Summary and Analysis of "Still Lives"

This chapter centers on Sandra's early love of drawing, which she loses after a traumatic incident with a famous sculptor on the Island, Don José. Don José and his German wife Doña Charito met in the Prado in Madrid. The two artists decided to move to the Island and settle in the outskirts of the capital in a "Hansel and Gretel" cottage. Sandra has shown a talent for drawing that distinguishes her, and so is given art lessons with Doña Charito. Superstition endows drawing with a magic-like power: a servant, Milagros, begs Sandra to destroy a picture she drew of Milagros' baby after the child comes down with fever; the next day, the baby is cured. After Sandra is forced to erase cats she has drawn on a stucco wall, the cellar is overrun by rats. The family decides to take Sandra to Doña Charito for art lessons, with thirteen of her girl cousins in tow.

At her first lesson, Sandra aches to begin drawing while Doña Charito lectures them. Her active imagination makes her perception of the world vibrant and emotionally charged. These perceptions, in turn, create a lush inner world inside that she years to release on paper. Doña Charito, however, for all her artistic expertise, does not recognize this passion. When Sandra ignores the lecture and begins to draw, Doña Charito charges her with impudence and commands her to sit in a punishment chair in another room.

Sandra, growing bored, wanders through the house and hears a man cursing from outside. Following the sound, she finds a locked shed and peers inside, thinking that she can revenge herself on Doña Charito by discovering one of the woman's secrets. Inside, she sees huge logs with half-formed creatures emerging from them. Then she sees a small man, naked and chained by the neck to an iron ring by the door, working on a sculpture of a woman with a spiked halo. He clambers on top of the sculpture, sexually aroused, and prepares to begin forming the woman's face.

Sandra cries out instinctively to warn the woman, and the man sees her and lunges towards the window. Sandra, who has been standing on a log, throws herself backwards, breaking her arm. The man appears at the window and studies her terrified face, her eyes riveted to his and her mouth screaming voicelessly. Then she begins to scream and he disappears; soon Doña Charito and the cousins come running, and find Sandra sobbing over her broken arm. She does not relate what she saw inside the shed.

With her arm in a cast, Sandra can no longer attend art lessons. By the time the cast comes off, months of pampering and the ridicule of jealous cousins have changed Sandra. She has turned inward, become sullen and dependent on her mother's attention. She no longer feels the urge to draw. That Christmas, she goes to a nativity pageant at the National Cathedral. The new crèche, unveiled that night, is composed of the giant creatures Sandra had seen in Don José's studio. Don José had finally finished the enormous project, and Sandra realizes that the Virgin Mary's face, wide-eyed in wonder, has been modeled from her own terrified face, which Don José had seen from the window of his shed.

Analysis

The chronology of Sandra's stories moves in a direct line backward from her breakdown, and almost all of them mention her dissatisfaction and unfulfilled inner hunger. Her stories seem focused on unraveling the mystery of her mental illness. This is the first chapter, however, in which Sandra speaks in the first person. She explicitly admits to having been altered for the worse by the experience of being pampered while her arm healed. This change seems to have provoked her later reliance on external sources of comfort, which are never fully adequate to her inner need.

Throughout the novel, Sandra has appeared as an unhappy woman who is unsatisfied by possessions, success, work, good looks, or sex. Her eating disorder and mental collapse are linked to this emptiness and lack of meaningful goals. This episode offers a clue as to how she came to be disconnected from the outside world. Her love of drawing is described in terms of creatures, spaces, even worlds that fill her imagination and seem to be "inside" of her. She can bring these things to life and relieve some of her metaphoric inward pressure by drawing.

The metaphor of another world residing within her implies a way for her to achieve satisfaction and happiness without external crutches. After she breaks her arm, however, she begins to turn inward, and is no longer willing or able to draw her internal world out. The pun in the phrase "draw it out" (254) signals the importance of drawing as the bridge between the external world and Sandra's inner creativity. Instead, Sandra becomes dependent on her mother's attention, beginning a cycle of neediness that leaves her perpetually unsatisfied.

Initiations into the sexual and social adult worlds are also central themes in this chapter. She watches Don José become sexually aroused while sculpting, implying that Sandra's excitement while drawing may have sexual sources she is unaware of. In addition, as a child, Sandra is painfully aware of her anonymity and her mortality. Constantly surrounded by a flock of cousins, she senses that she has no purpose except as another vehicle of the illustrious de la Torre family name. This premature awareness of her social role reveals the same sensitivity to social relations that she shows in her keen observations of the Fannings. She is also preoccupied with power dynamics. She looks into the shed in order to take revenge on Doña Charito, recognizing that knowing a secret about someone will enable her to control him.

Finally, the chapter explores the meaning of creativity. As a child, Sandra's sees in terms of vivid metaphors that transform mundane things into active, vibrant creatures. For instance, she sees Doña Charito's tongue "like some fat beast caged inside her mouth" (245). Her creative talent is not simply in copying images accurately on paper, but making them come alive through her active imagination.

Sandra's sensual, lively vision aligns with the superstitious Dominican attitude towards art and drawing. Milagros' belief that Sandra's drawing has afflicted her child with fever is connected to Sandra's sensation of bringing cats and birds to life by drawing them. The joy Sandra takes in the act of creation is perhaps the element missing from her unsatisfied adult life.

Summary and Analysis of "Still Lives"

Summary and Analysis of "An American Surprise"

In this chapter, Carla recounts an episode from her childhood in the Dominican Republic, just after Sofía's birth. Her father has recently returned from a visit to New York. He always brings surprise presents for the girls from F.A.O. Schwarz, and this year has brought each of them a cast-iron mechanical bank for holding pennies. Sandra's bank is a girl who jumps rope when a penny is inserted, Yolanda's is a bank of Jonah and the whale, and Carla's bank is a figure of the Virgin Mary ascending to Heaven.

The family has a new pantry maid, Gladys, who wants to move to New York and become a famous actress. She is deeply Catholic, and calls the Statue of Liberty the "American Virgin" (260), a saint that will help Gladys find her way to New York. Gladys is riveted by the mechanical ascension of the Virgin Mary bank.

A few weeks later, Christmas comes. Carla receives a baby doll that cries and drinks, and soon forgets the now-broken Virgin Mary bank. Gladys, who receives a leather wallet from the family for Christmas, comes into Carla's room that night and offers to buy the bank. Since it is broken, Carla decides to give her the bank for free, but is worried that giving away her father's present will bring punishment on them both, so warns Gladys not to tell her parents.

Soon, however, her mother notices the missing bank. When Carla tells her that she does not know where it is, Laura looks through the servants' quarters and finds it. Gladys is dismissed, and her sobbing prompts a confession from Carla. Laura hurries off to explain the misunderstanding to the other servants and clear Gladys' name, but the damage has already been done to Gladys' standing in the house, and she asks to leave. In the final scene, Carla sits on her father's lap as he looks sadly at the Virgin Mary bank. They insert a penny to watch her rise, but the lever jams and the Virgin remains stuck halfway up.

Analysis

When Gladys is dismissed, the truth of her innocence emerges too late to save her standing in the household. The story's outcome reveals the unsentimental reality of Dominican class relations, in which a simple misunderstanding can significantly alter or damage the life of a subordinate. The final, failed ascension of the mechanical Virgin Mary bank is a symbol for entrapment in a rigid social hierarchy that allows little or no upward mobility.

In particular, the image offers an allegory for the probable failure of Gladys's dream of becoming a famous actress in New York. Gladys associates New York with the Virgin, calling the Statue of Liberty a "powerful American Virgin." The stalled ascension symbolizes the probable failure of both Gladys' dream and her hope for miraculous intervention from the saints. Class relations are maintained so strictly that there is little likelihood Gladys will ever leave the Island or even rise above a pantry maid. At the same time, her superstitious practices, mixing desire for personal gain with religion, will not actually help her achieve fame in New York.

The Catholicism of the servants is laced with superstition. They light candles and keep figures of saints for various sorts of luck, practices reminiscent of Chucha's voodoo. Gladys speaks of saints as though they were tools to help her accomplish things, such as earning money or protecting one's eyesight. When the mechanized Virgin rises, Gladys looks as though she were seeing an actual miracle, prompting Carlos's patronizing remark that the servants are "like children" (266). Gladys seems to mistake the ingenuity of human craftsmanship for divine intervention, demonstrating the mixture of materialism and religious belief that produces superstition. Although less superstitious than the servants, the García family also focuses on the material aspects of Christian holidays, such as presents, decorations, parties and food during Christmas.

The chapter also explores the relations between masters and servants in a Dominican household. The servants often grumble about their workload, while Carlos and Laura treat them with firm discipline and patronizing kindness. The servants mix deference with criticism and complaint in their behavior towards their masters. The uneasy dynamic interferes with even the most pleasant conversation, prompting condescension on one side and grumbling on the other.

The question of moral behavior, whether according to religion, social hierarchy, or family obedience proves more complicated in this story than the rigid rules of the society allow. When Gladys asks to buy Carla's bank, Carla struggles to reach the right decision. The moral rules dictated by her mother contradict each other in this case, and Carla senses that giving the bank away and keeping it are both partly good and partly wrong actions. She wonders how "being good worked" (270), as though morality is also mechanized and will respond if you press the correct lever. In dismissing Gladys, the Garcías initially think they are doing right to turn out a thief. However, when they learn the whole story, the moral rules no longer operate in so clear a fashion. Even after her innocence is declared, Gladys has still been shamed before her peers, and she chooses to leave rather than face the contempt of the household. No simple way exists to determine the right course of action for the Garcías or Gladys, and the moral system seems to have broken down just like the mechanical bank.

Summary and Analysis of "The Drum"

The final chapter of the novel is told in the first person by Yolanda about herself as a young girl. Her grandmother, whom she calls Mamita, brings a toy drum to the Dominican Republic from F.A.O. Schwarz in New York. Yolanda wanders around the yard for weeks playing her drum, even after she loses both drumsticks and must play with dowel rods.

While playing outside, Yolanda also likes to visit the coal shed at the back of the property, which has become haunted for all the children. A Haitian laundry maid, Pila, who practiced voodoo, warned her that all the local spirits and devils lived in the coal shed. Pila was only employed by the family a few months before she ran away with ten shopping bags of stolen clothing. She was caught and the clothing returned, but she still left her mark on the property in the form of the haunted shed. By the time Yolanda receives her drum, Pila has been gone a few weeks but has left a haunted coal shed behind.

Yolanda, a tomboy and daredevil, decides to go into the coal shed alone one day. As she looks into the barrels of coal, she finds a litter of kittens, but no mother in sight. Yolanda picks a kitten with white paws as her favorite and names him Schwarz after the toy store, but leaves the coal shed without him, afraid that the mother will attack her if she finds Yolanda there. On her return to the house, Yolanda meets a strange man with a gun strapped to his back and a big dog named Kashtanka. The man warns Yolanda that the kitten may die if she takes it from its mother too early, and suggests she wait at least seven days, until Thursday. The two see the mother cat go into the shed and come out again, and once the man has left, Yolanda sneaks back into the shed to look at Schwarz.

While in the shed, she hears a report from the man's gun coming from the orange grove, and realizes he is hunting birds. An intuition of adult hypocrisy dawns on Yolanda, who thinks of all the baby birds the man is leaving orphaned by his shooting. Without pausing to consider her action, she grabs Schwarz from the coal bin and runs out of the shed with him. Seeing the mother cat sunning herself, Yolanda grows frightened and slips the Schwarz into her toy drum. She marches by the mother, banging feverishly on the drum to muffle the kitten's plaintive meowing.

Once Yolanda reaches the safety of her house, she tosses Schwarz out of the window and, afraid of the mother cat's retaliation, watches from inside all morning as the hurt kitten tries to limp back to the coal shed. That night, Yolanda wakes up to see the mother cat perched at the foot of her bed. She discovers the next day that the new laundry maid, Nivea, left a window open that night. However, the cat continues to return even after the windows have been securely shut.

For months and even years after, Yolanda is haunted by visions of the mother cat. Yolanda ends the chapter by addressing the reader directly to explain why she is telling the story. She describes herself as a curious woman, fascinated by ghost stories, and suffering from bad dreams and bad insomnia. All of these qualities, she implies, and even her urge to write, stem from this disturbing episode.

Analysis

In some ways, this chapter does not bring much closure to the novel, since it does not explicitly address central themes such as immigration, language, sexuality, or the political situation. The chapter deals with an apparently trivial incident in Yolanda's childhood. However, Yolanda's overwhelming, inarticulate guilt at her action haunts her in the form of a sinister cat that comes to affect her psychological life for the rest of her life.

In the story, Yolanda cannot fully articulate some of the abstract feelings and ideas she has. For instance, she recognizes that the poacher is violating his own rule by killing birds in the orange grove, but she has no word for "hypocrisy." She does not admit to any feelings of guilt after taking Schwarz, and only mentions her fear of being attacked by the mother. However, her initially selfish fears seem to transform into moral pangs of their own accord. She later recognizes the vision of the cat as an embodiment of guilt—of her reaction to the "violation" (290) she perpetrated on Schwarz and its mother.

The accumulated effect of these visions is anxiety, insomnia and the excitement of an already active imagination. These psychological disturbances impel her to write poems and stories as a means of understanding her anxieties and fears. She writes to pick apart and understand her past, as she explains in "The Rudy Elmenhurst Story." The vision of the cat therefore becomes the driving force behind her whole creative life.

The final chapter, seemingly disconnected from the previous tales, thus represents a final stage in Yolanda's struggle to find the root of her compulsion to write. This discovery encapsulates a vital current underlying the novel—the purpose of storytelling. The novel's reversed chronology supports the idea of storytelling as a way to work backwards through one's life and recognize underlying patterns. For Yolanda, this process seems to culminate with the explanation of the cat's enduring impact on her life.

Yolanda even remarks on the relation between real life and storytelling in the chapter. When she hears the man shooting in the orange grove, she comments that one can "call it coincidence, call it plot" (286) that such an event would occur and affect her actions. Real life and storytelling become tangled, and what was originally coincidence becomes plot in retrospect. The same is true of the vision of the mother cat, whose appearance on the first night is probably simple coincidence, but who transforms the plot of Yolanda's life.

The black cat becomes a symbol of the unresolved emotions that compel Yolanda to write. She practices her art in order to tame and understand these feelings and their effect on her. The cat can be a violent, wild, and uncontrollable animal. As a symbol, it suggests a fierce, irrational, and mute energy that Yolanda can subdue only by putting it into words and fitting into it the pattern of her life. Nevertheless, the powerful final image f the black cat with its howling magenta mouth hints that the cat can never be fully tamed. It will always lurk in corners of her unconscious where her rational mind cannot reach, driving her onwards.

Suggested Essay Questions

1. **Discuss Yolanda's relationship to language. Why is she so sensitive to English and how does this quality affect her romantic relationships?**

As a poet and the novel's primary narrator, Yolanda has the closest and most troubled relation to language. Because she learns English as a second language, Yolanda develops an ear sensitive to the musicality of the words. However, she also finds that her inability to use English casually or crudely contributes to stiffness in her interactions. She often speaks in rhyme or creates surreal images based on how words sound together, releasing an immense creative energy that her partners cannot seem to match. She seeks a romantic partner with a similar sensitivity to words, believing that reverence for language indicates respect for the thing spoken about (for instance, sex, and by extension, herself). The intensity of Yolanda's relation to language nurses an uneasy relativism in her, so that she resists the notion that the outside world is more "real" or meaningful than her surreal poetic visions.

2. **Why is Carlos so morose during his 70th birthday party? What does his bitterness suggest about his relation to his daughters and wife, and about the conflict between Dominican and American cultural ideals?**

Carlos's birthday is traditionally considered a special time during which the girls visit their father without their husbands, and he gives them stacks of cash with his name signed on the top bill. His emphasis on exerting masculine control over them and providing for them economically derives from his deeply held belief in the traditional Dominican family structure. At the party, he begins to realize that his daughters and even his wife are in no way materially dependent on him, as Dominican women are expected to be. They have pursued an ideal of American individuality and independence. However, he fails to recognize that he can still influence and enrich their emotional lives, even if they do not need his money.

3. **The García girls undergo puberty while still adapting to life in the United States. In what ways does their displacement into a foreign language and culture affect or relate to their new sexual awareness?**

Both Carla and Yolanda remark that they learn many sexual terms in English before knowing their Spanish equivalents. Their rude, frightening awakening into sexuality is thus linked with their sudden immersion in an uncomfortable language. Carla feels that both events brand her as an outsider. Yolanda similarly traces both her overly formal, cautious English and her initial wariness of sex back to her immigrant roots. Though all four girls undergo some form of the same experience, Sandra is apparently protected by her attractive, Caucasian looks, while Sofía has more time to grow into English and American culture than her sisters do.

4. **Pick two or three of these central themes and explain how they intersect and influence each other in the novel: language, sexuality/gender, rebellion, family, and storytelling.**

Answers will vary. Language and sexuality, for instance, are linked for Carla and Yolanda, who face an uneasy awakening into sexuality and an uncomfortable new language at the same time. Both sexual and political rebellions beset the García family: just as the family fled to the States for freedom from oppression, so the girls escape the tyranny of a patriarchal family by embracing the sexual revolution. Storytelling is a way of celebrating each girl's uniqueness while affirming the family's unity and shared values. Many other combinations are possible. It may help to focus on how two themes parallel each other and where they diverge.

5. **Laura García is an inveterate storyteller who loves to relate tales about her daughters to family, friends, and strangers alike. What is the significance of her habit of storytelling? How does it reflect the family dynamic and her own relationship with her daughters?**

Each of Laura's stories captures some idiosyncrasy that characterizes a person or a time period. While serving as markers of individuality, the stories also provide a communal history that unites the family despite sometimes conflicting convictions. The stories are also significant for what Laura chooses to emphasize or leave out. She sometimes sanitizes her stories by eliminating unpleasant parts, such as ignoring the battle between Sofía and her father when discussing Sofía's marriage. By altering the story to suit herself, Laura indicates her unwillingness to confront points of tension, such as her daughters' sexuality, disobedience, and nervous breakdowns. For this question, you may want to choose stories about a certain daughter, or stories that share a theme or set of characteristics.

6. **Consider the novel's structure. What is the effect of subtitling each chapter with the name(s) of its central character(s)? Why does Alvarez choose to narrate some chapters in first person and others in third, some in future tense and others in the narrative present? How do these elements affect the reader's perception of the García family dynamic? You may focus on one chapter or choose to discuss multiple examples of a particular narrative technique.**

This is a complicated question with many possible responses. Choosing two or three chapters at most is recommended. You may want to discuss, for instance, why some of Yolanda's chapters are narrated in first person and others in third, and how this difference relates to the themes or purpose of each chapter. In addition, you might consider why "A Regular Revolution" is written in the first person plural ("we") without any individual, designated narrator. In general, think about how Alvarez establishes the relationships among the characters using these narrative techniques.

7. **Each girl, with the possible exception of Sofía, undergoes some traumatic event early in life. Consider one or more of the sisters and discuss how her/their personality or outlook was changed by a formative childhood event. How are these narratives constructed? You may also choose to discuss why Sofía's integration into American culture is largely skipped over and how her development differs from that of her sisters.**

Carla encounters a pervert and a gang of racist boys on the playground; Sandra breaks her arm after taking fright at Don José, and becomes needy and dependent on external affirmation after months of isolation and pampering; Yolanda recounts having night terrors after stealing a kitten from its mother. The sisters either state or imply that these events shape their future lives: Carla becomes a child psychologist, Sandra an unsatisfied and unhappy woman, and Yolanda an imaginative, uneasy writer who narrates in order to understand unresolved emotions and failures. By beginning with the sisters as full-fledged adults and moving backwards, the novel traces their development retrospectively, which is the only way patterns can be drawn from the events that compose a life. Although these specific incidents may not have been solely responsible for the sisters' personalities, it is telling that the girls identify these events as worth recounting.

8. **Sofía narrates only one chapter in the novel, yet much of the story revolves around her. Think about why Sofía is largely silent in the novel, and how her development reflects on that of her sisters. How does she both reject and conform to American and Dominican culture?**

By dropping out of college and then eloping, Sofía rejects the ambition and materialistic aspects of American culture at the same time that she violates deeply rooted Dominican family values. Her fiercely independent spirit leaves her apparently the least successful of the sisters: she has no advanced degree and no real career. However, she is the only sister with no history of divorces, a healthy family life, and children. Her family-oriented life and the birth of her son bring her closer to filling the traditional Dominican female role than her sisters. Yet she seems uninterested in conforming to any model, and appears to act on a set of personal principles—though the reader is left to guess at what these are, being offered little firsthand insight into her decisions.

9. **Discuss the tension between Dominican and American cultural ideals with which the García sisters must struggle. For instance, how are sexual morality and rebellion viewed differently in American and Dominican culture? Do Dominican family values conflict with the American emphasis on individuality and independence?**

American society in the novel encourages each girl to nurture her strengths, pursue higher education and a meaningful career. This cultural milieu, informed by 1960s and 70s feminism, favors sexual exploration and teaches women to seek satisfaction outside the home and family. Even their mother Laura is affected, seizing the chance to take adult courses in business management and real estate. Such rebellion, as Yolanda discovers when reading Whitman, is considered the engine of American progress. However, this emphasis on individual achievement jeopardizes the family unity central to Dominican culture. Of the daughters, only Sofía, who has rejected the ambitious, upwardly mobile aspects of American culture, has children and a settled family life. Yet she too has broken the familial hierarchy of Dominican society by eloping. Each sister strikes an uneasy balance between the two cultures.

10. **In the novel's last paragraph, Yolanda sketches out the story of her life so that it fits in the "hollow" of her story. What does this novel tell you about the relation between real life and storytelling? In what ways is storytelling helpful and/or inadequate to the task of understanding personal development? It may help you to think about how the novel is structured.**

Stories provide an immersive experience that offers more emotional information than bare facts do. However, stories are not real life, but are composed of details selected by the teller to form a pattern. The attempt to understand a life requires drawing out such patterns in retrospect, and storytelling may help the teller recognize them. The reverse chronology of the novel allows the reader—like a storyteller—to examine the cause-and-effect operating in the sisters' lives. In her final paragraph, Yolanda admits that many characters in the chapter "The Drum" have little or no direct influence on her life. However, by focusing on seemingly trivial events in this final chapter, Yolanda reminds us that the events that shape a life are not always easy to identify.

The Trujillo Era

Rafael Leónidas Trujillo Molina (1891-1961), commonly called Trujillo and nicknamed El Jefe (The Boss), ruled the Dominican Republic from 1930 until his assassination in 1961. Though only officially president from 1930 to 1938 and from 1942 to 1952, he maintained absolute power as a *caudillo*, or military strongman, with puppet presidents drawn from his circle of family and close friends.

Trujillo first gained prominence when he rose through the ranks of the U.S. constabulary army established to occupy the Dominican Republic from 1916 to 1924 and prevent the D.R. from defaulting on foreign debts. When the U.S. Marines left the island in 1924, Trujillo was named a top military commander. In February of 1930, Trujillo cooperated with a coup to overthrow then-President Horacio Vásquez. Trujillo then ran for president with the newly formed Dominican Party and won on May 16 with 95% of the vote, an absurd figure later proved to be fraudulent. He was 38 years old when he took office on August 16, wearing a sash with the motto "Dios y Trujillo" ("God and Trujillo"). He requested the congress to declare his term the "Trujillo Era" and immediately assumed dictatorial powers. In 1931, he made the Dominican Party the sole legal political party, although it was already known that those who did not join the Party risked reprisals. Anyone without a Party membership card could be charged with vagrancy, and opponents of the regime were mysteriously killed or disappeared. Trujillo encouraged a cult of personality surrounding him, including changing the capital's name from Santiago to Ciudad Trujillo in 1936, and popularizing the slogan "Dios en cielo, Trujillo en tierra" ("God in Heaven, Trujillo on earth.")

In 1958, Johnny Abbes García became head of the newly created Military Intelligence Service (SIM), a secret police notorious for murders at home and assassination attempts abroad. Most notably, the SIM twice tried to assassinate the Venezuelan president Rómulo Betancourt, and it was strongly condemned by the Organization of American States (OAS). The 1960 murder of the Mirabal sisters, active opponents of the regime, is the subject of Julia Alvarez's novel *In the Time of the Butterflies* (1994).

Trujillo exercised an open-door policy that favored Caucasian immigrants including Jewish refugees during WWII and Spanish immigrants after the Spanish Civil War. However, he developed a particular, virulent breed of racism, anti-Haitianism, directed against the Dominican Republic's darker-skinned neighbors who share the island of Hispaniola. Suppressing his own partial Haitian descent, Trujillo accused Haiti of harboring his opponents and ordered a massacre on the Haitian border. The Parsley Massacre of October 1937 left an estimated 20,000 to 30,000 Haitians dead. In *How the García Girls Lost their Accents*, the de la Torres have a Haitian maid, Chucha, who arrives at their doorstep seeking asylum after having survived the massacre. Trujillo wanted a war with Haiti, hoping to defeat them and gain control of the entire island of Hispaniola, but Haiti responded by requesting an international investigation. Eventually, the Dominican Republic was required to pay a paltry sum in reparations to the victims' families, most of which was embezzled by corrupt Haitian officials.

On May 30, 1961, Trujillo was fatally shot in an assassination plot carried out by Dominican conspirators. There is strong evidence that the CIA was involved in planning and executing the plot. Trujillo's rule left the Dominican Republic with a vast infrastructure and more stability and prosperity than most living Dominicans had previously known. However, this economic advancement came at a huge cost to civil liberties and human rights.

Author of ClassicNote and Sources

Mai Wang, author of ClassicNote. Completed on September 10, 2010, copyright held by GradeSaver.

Updated and revised Bella Wang September 29, 2010. Copyright held by GradeSaver.

Alvarez, Julia. How the Garcia Girls Lost Their Accents. Chapel Hill: Algonquin Books of Chapel Hill, 2010.

Alvarez, Julia. In the Time of the Butterflies. New York: Plume, 1995.

Sirias, Silvio. Julia Alvarez: A Critical Companion (Critical Companions to Popular Contemporary Writers). Westport, CT: Greenwood Press, 2001.

Sáez, Elena Machado, and Raphael Dalleo. The Latino/a Canon and the Emergence of Post-Sixties Literature. New York: Palgrave Macmillan, 2007.

Luis, William. "A Search for Identity in Julia Alvarez's How the García Girls Lost Their Accents." *Callaloo*. Volume 23, Number 3, Summer 2000, pp. 839-849.

Castells, Ricardo. "The silence of exile in *How the Garcia Girls Lost Their Accents*." *Bilingual Review*. Vol. 26, 2001.

Quiz 1

1. **Why do Tio Orlando and Tio Ignacio agree to pass Manuel Gustavo off as Tio Ignacio's son?**
   A. Manuel Gustavo looks like Tio Ignacio
   B. To protect Tio Orlando's marriage and convince the relatives that Tio Ignacio isnâ—Žt gay
   C. Tio Ignacio is already a known as sexually loose, while Tio Orlando has a spotless reputation
   D. Manuel Gustavo likes Tio Ignacio better

2. **What three figures do the girls cite to display their feminism on the Island?**
   A. Virginia Woolf, Eudora Welty, Elizabeth Cady Stanton
   B. Virginia Woolf, Susan B. Anthony, Mary Wollstonecraft
   C. Eudora Welty, Cleopatra, Lakshmi
   D. Betty Friedan, Betsy Ross, Susan B. Anthony

3. **Why does Yolanda refuse to have sex with Rudy, both in college and after they graduate?**
   A. His irreverence towards language and sex makes her feel that he doesn't respect her
   B. She's afraid that she'll become pregnant
   C. He's not in love with her, and this breaks Yolanda's heart
   D. He never comes to class on time and makes him help her write his poems

4. **Why does Papi decide to become un dominican-york?**
   A. The food is better in New York.
   B. To flee the political instability and revolution in the Dominican Republic
   C. He was in the dictatorâ—Žs inner circle.
   D. The United States had more opportunities for his daughters.

5. **How did Mami differentiate the daughters when they were young?**
   A. Each girl had her own color.
   B. Each girl had a special hairstyle.
   C. Each girl had her own special food.
   D. Each girl played a different instrument.

6. **What is Carla's opinion about the scheme Mami used to differentiate the girls when they were young?**
   A. She thinks children benefit from being placed into ordered regimes.
   B. She thinks it was a smart way to tell the daughters apart.
   C. She thinks it caused the daughters problems in differentiating

themselves.

    D. She thinks her mother shouldnâ—Žt have tried to tell them apart.

7. **How is Sandra different from her sisters?**
    A. She is the only one who won't eat pasta.
    B. She is the only one interested in boys.
    C. She is the only one to see a psychiatrist.
    D. She is the only one with blue eyes and light skin.

8. **What is a symptom of Sandra's breakdown?**
    A. She thinks sheâ—Žs a monkey.
    B. She burned her bra.
    C. She hallucinates.
    D. She is a chronic liar.

9. **How does Sofía offend her father on his birthday?**
    A. She wonâ—Žt let him talk to his grandchildren.
    B. She arouses him in public by kissing his ear.
    C. She accuses him of tyranny and misogyny.
    D. She refuses to kiss him goodnight.

10. **How did Carla and her husband, the analyst, meet?**
    A. At a psychiatric convention.
    B. He was her analyst after her first marriage.
    C. Carla was the psychiatrist for his children.
    D. At a bar.

11. **Why are Sofía and her father on bad terms?**
    A. She ran away after he discovered her love letters.
    B. He found her marijuana.
    C. She refused to go to boarding school.
    D. She refused to marry the man he chose.

12. **What words give Yolanda an allergic reaction?**
    A. Doctor, Yolanda
    B. love, alive
    C. Yolanda, sex
    D. spirit, love

13. **What is the primary symptom of Yolanda's breakdown?**
    A. She is incapable of falling in love.
    B. She quotes literature compulsively.
    C. She refuses to eat.
    D. She thinks she is a monkey.

14. **What is Papi's favorite saying?**
    A. "Good bulls sire cows."
    B. "Curiosity killed the cat."
    C. "Girls should be seen, never heard."
    D. "A bird in the hand is worth two in the bush."

15. **What is the title of the list belonging to John that Yolanda finds?**
    A. for-and-against-slash-Joe-slash-wife
    B. women-I-love-slash-hate
    C. to live-slash-die
    D. for-and-against-slash-Joe-slash-divorce

16. **What is the main difference between Yolanda's first love sonnet and Rudy's?**
    A. Her sonnet is elevated while his is full of sexual references.
    B. Hers is personal while his is generic.
    C. The class likes hers but finds his offensive.
    D. Her sonnet rhymes and his doesnâ—Žt.

17. **Why does Manuel Gustavo refuse to wear a condom?**
    A. He thinks it will make him infertile.
    B. He thinks it makes him look ugly.
    C. He wants to have a child with Fifi and marry her.
    D. He loves Fifi.

18. **What happens when Yolanda meets the two men in Altamira?**
    A. They speak rudely to her but donâ—Žt hurt her.
    B. They fix her tires and demand payment.
    C. They fix her tires and refuse payment.
    D. They kidnap her and steal her car.

19. **What is Yolanda's main problem with Rudy Elmenhurst?**
    A. He uses coarse language to talk about sex.
    B. He doesnâ—Žt respect her Catholic upbringing.
    C. He wonâ—Žt write poems about her.
    D. He wonâ—Žt wear a condom.

20. **What word best describes Yolanda in high school?**
    A. Beautiful
    B. Vivacious
    C. Aloof
    D. Ditzy

21. **What is the name of the hospital Sandra is sent to?**
    A. Our Lady of Mercy
    B. Mount Hope
    C. Mayo Clinic
    D. Payne Clinic

22. **What is the father's main demand on his birthday each year?**
    A. That the girls bring him gifts.
    B. That the girls come without their husbands.
    C. That the girls help their mother cook.
    D. That the girls not wear make-up or perfume when they arrive.

23. **What did Mami call the four girls when they were young?**
    A. Cuquita
    B. Amorcita
    C. Chiquita
    D. Cutie

24. **What is the name of Fifi's husband?**
    A. Manuel Gustavo
    B. Rudy Elmenhurst
    C. Otto
    D. Clive

25. **Who wrote the autobiographical paper "I Was There Too" and what was it about?**
    A. Sandi wrote it about struggling with mental disorder
    B. Carla wrote it about her mother's child-rearing techniques
    C. Yolanda wrote it about trying to become a poet
    D. Papi wrote it about fighting in the Revolution on the Island

Quiz 1 Answer Key

1. **(B)** To protect Tio Orlando's marriage and convince the relatives that Tio Ignacio isn't gay
2. **(B)** Virginia Woolf, Susan B. Anthony, Mary Wollstonecraft
3. **(A)** His irreverence towards language and sex makes her feel that he doesn't respect her
4. **(B)** To flee the political instability and revolution in the Dominican Republic
5. **(A)** Each girl had her own color.
6. **(C)** She thinks it caused the daughters problems in differentiating themselves.
7. **(D)** She is the only one with blue eyes and light skin.
8. **(A)** She thinks she's a monkey.
9. **(B)** She arouses him in public by kissing his ear.
10. **(B)** He was her analyst after her first marriage.
11. **(A)** She ran away after he discovered her love letters.
12. **(B)** love, alive
13. **(B)** She quotes literature compulsively.
14. **(A)** "Good bulls sire cows."
15. **(A)** for-and-against-slash-Joe-slash-wife
16. **(A)** Her sonnet is elevated while his is full of sexual references.
17. **(A)** He thinks it will make him infertile.
18. **(C)** They fix her tires and refuse payment.
19. **(A)** He uses coarse language to talk about sex.
20. **(B)** Vivacious
21. **(B)** Mount Hope
22. **(B)** That the girls come without their husbands.
23. **(A)** Cuquita
24. **(C)** Otto
25. **(B)** Carla wrote it about her mother's child-rearing techniques

Quiz 2

1. **What is Carla's profession?**
   - A. Child psychologist
   - B. Pediatrician
   - C. Schoolteacher
   - D. Psychoanalyst

2. **Why does Fifi have to spend a year on the Island?**
   - A. Mami wants her to appreciate her opportunities in the States.
   - B. Mami found out about her boyfriends.
   - C. Mami found her bag of marijuana.
   - D. Papi wants her to respect his authority more fully.

3. **Who is Clive?**
   - A. A handsome relation of Otto's.
   - B. Sandi's psychiatrist.
   - C. Yolanda's married lover.
   - D. A famous actor the girls love to gossip about.

4. **What is Otto's profession?**
   - A. Chemist
   - B. Analyst
   - C. Translator
   - D. Banker

5. **Why does Yolanda tell the story of Rudy Elmenhurst?**
   - A. She is bored and telling stories entertains her.
   - B. To teach other girls that they can have healthy relationships without sex.
   - C. To get revenge on him for insisting she have sex with him.
   - D. To understand for herself why she refused to sleep with Rudy.

6. **What animal haunts Yolanda as a child?**
   - A. A mouse.
   - B. A cat.
   - C. A bird.
   - D. A bull.

7. **Where does the cantina owner's son, Jose Duarte, Sanchez y Mella, get his names from?**
    A. Places in Spain where his ancestors originated.
    B. The names of his mother's ancestors.
    C. His father's relatives who were killed in the Revolution.
    D. The three national liberators.

8. **What does antojo mean?**
    A. Someone who betrays their country.
    B. A compulsive yearning.
    C. Eyeglasses.
    D. Someone with good vision.

9. **What does Mami read before going to bed?**
    A. The Bible.
    B. Romance novels.
    C. The New York Times.
    D. Dominican newspapers.The New Yor

10. **What poet inspires Yolanda's first draft of her Teacher's Day address in ninth grade?**
    A. Emily Dickinson
    B. Pablo Neruda
    C. Walt Whitman
    D. Robert Frost

11. **What invention of Mami's is patented by someone else first?**
    A. Washing machine with the prewash soak cycle.
    B. A rolling suitcase.
    C. A refrigerator with automatic defrost.
    D. A potty that plays music to help potty-train a toddler.

12. **What does Papi buy for Yolanda to ask her forgiveness after tearing her speech up?**
    A. A fountain pen.
    B. A new dress.
    C. A lock for her door.
    D. A typewriter.

13. **Why does Papi begin to consider moving back to the Island when Yolanda is in ninth grade?**

A. The dictator has been toppled and the secret police are offering amnesty to political opponents.

B. He fears his wife is growing too liberal-minded and Americanized.

C. The interim government is holding free elections for the first time in thirty years.

D. The girls are too old to continue living in a foreign culture.

14. **What major event of the Cold War occurs while Yolanda is in fourth grade?**

A. The Watergate Scandal (1972).

B. The first man walks on the moon (1969).

C. The Cuban Missile Crisis (1962).

D. The Tet Offensive (1968).

15. **When Yolanda first sees snow, what does she mistake it for?**

A. She thinks it's radioactive fallout from an atomic bomb.

B. She thinks the sky is falling.

C. She knows it's snow, since she saw it on the Island once before.

D. She thinks it's confetti from a parade outside.

16. **What is the "magical store" that Mamita visits in the United States?**

A. Barnes and Noble

B. FAO Schwarz

C. RadioShack

D. Prada

17. **Why did the Dominican maids fear Pila, the old laundry maid?**

A. They thought her splotched skin was contagious.

B. She scolded them often.

C. She was Haitian, which was synonymous with voodoo to them.

D. They thought her missing eye was magic.

18. **What does Yoyo name the kitten she wants to adopt?**

A. Mamita

B. Yolanda

C. New York

D. Schwarz

19. **Why does the girls' grandfather not surround his yard with a fence?**
A. He doesnâ—Žt want to offend the dictator, Trujillo, whose family lives adjacent to him.
B. It will be useless to keep the poachers out.
C. He cannot afford to.
D. He wants the poor to be able to enter his grounds and receive charity.

20. **Why does Yoyo conclude with the episode about the kitten she smuggles in her toy drum?**
A. It illustrates her youthful cruelty and guilt.
B. All of her sisters were present when it happened.
C. It helps to explain her insomnia and fascination with ghost stories, even as an adult.
D. Itâ—Žs the most exciting of her memories.

21. **What does Carla see while walking home from school?**
A. A pervert.
B. A rabid dog.
C. A man being robbed.
D. A prostitute.

22. **Why does Sister Zoe give Yolanda a special seat in the front of her class?**
A. Because she thinks Yolanda is smarter than the other students.
B. To single Yolanda out as an immigrant.
C. So she can reprimand her.
D. So she can tutor her separately.

23. **What is the name of the restaurant that the Garcias and Fannings visit?**
A. Flor de Espana
B. El Matador
C. El Flamenco
D. El Toreador

24. **Why does Sandra want the doll dressed like a flamenco dancer?**
A. It reminds her of the beauty and passion of her culture.
B. She thinks it looks like her.
C. She wants to show her friends at school what Spanish dresses look like.
D. She wants revenge on Mami for being so strict.

25. Where does Carlos hide from the SIM?
  A. In a secret room underground.
  B. In the orange grove.
  C. Under the bed.
  D. In a secret room behind the closet.

Quiz 2 Answer Key

1. **(A)** Child psychologist
2. **(C)** Mami found her bag of marijuana.
3. **(C)** Yolanda's married lover.
4. **(A)** Chemist
5. **(D)** To understand for herself why she refused to sleep with Rudy.
6. **(B)** A cat.
7. **(D)** The three national liberators.
8. **(B)** A compulsive yearning.
9. **(C)** The New York Times.
10. **(C)** Walt Whitman
11. **(B)** A rolling suitcase.
12. **(D)** A typewriter.
13. **(C)** The interim government is holding free elections for the first time in thirty years.
14. **(C)** The Cuban Missile Crisis (1962).
15. **(A)** She thinks it's radioactive fallout from an atomic bomb.
16. **(B)** FAO Schwarz
17. **(C)** She was Haitian, which was synonymous with voodoo to them.
18. **(D)** Schwarz
19. **(A)** He doesn't want to offend the dictator, Trujillo, whose family lives adjacent to him.
20. **(C)** It helps to explain her insomnia and fascination with ghost stories, even as an adult.
21. **(A)** A pervert.
22. **(D)** So she can tutor her separately.
23. **(C)** El Flamenco
24. **(A)** It reminds her of the beauty and passion of her culture.
25. **(D)** In a secret room behind the closet.

Quiz 3

1. **Where did Dona Charito and Don Jose meet?**
    A. An art museum in Germany
    B. The Prado in Spain
    C. The Louvre in Paris
    D. While painting on a beach in Spain

2. **What does Sandi see inside the shed at Dona Charito's house?**
    A. A naked man with a chain around his neck, sculpting an enormous chariot.
    B. A naked man with a chain around his neck, sculpting the Virgin Mary.
    C. A naked man dancing around a statue of the Virgin Mary.
    D. A room full of enormous marble statues.

3. **Who is Yolanda's best friend as a child?**
    A. She plays by herself
    B. Mundin
    C. Lucinda
    D. Carmencita

4. **Why does the gardener look frightened whenever the adults call for him?**
    A. He's afraid the guardia have come to take him.
    B. He has a limp leg and cannot walk very quickly.
    C. He's afraid the family has discovered his marijuana plants.
    D. He's worried that the children have told about his pornographic magazine.

5. **Why does Papito travel to New York?**
    A. He works for a bank based in New York
    B. He has a post with the United Nations
    C. He likes to travel
    D. He wants to visit his family in New York

6. **Why does the family pity Tia Mimi?**
    A. She had a miscarriage
    B. She has an ugly skin condition
    C. They think she is too educated to marry
    D. They think she is a lesbian

7. **How does Papi get red sneakers for Carla?**
    A. He asks Tio Mundo to smuggle a pair from the States.
    B. He paints sneakers red with lipstick.
    C. He paints sneakers red with nailpolish.
    D. He works overtime to pay for them.

8. **What is Sandi's favorite toy as a girl?**
    A. A snowglobe with a little red house.
    B. She doesn't have a favorite toy.
    C. The Human Body doll.
    D. Her mechanical bank.

9. **Who is Victor Hubbard?**
    A. The doorman at the Garcia's New York apartment building.
    B. A CIA agent in the Dominican Republic.
    C. One of Yolanda's friends from college.
    D. A SIM agent in New York.

10. **Why does Mami want Sofia to leave the Dominican Republic?**
    A. Mami wants her to have a better education.
    B. Mami thinks having a Dominican boyfriend is bad for Sofia
    C. Sofia was caught going off alone with her boyfriend.
    D. Mami doesn't approve of Manuel Gustavo.

11. **Which sister does not graduate college?**
    A. Sandra
    B. Yolanda
    C. Carla
    D. Sofia

12. **What does Yolanda call Papi after he tears her speech up?**
    A. Chapita
    B. Bastard
    C. Trujillo
    D. Il Duce

13. **How did Dr. Fanning help Carlos?**
   A. He secured a fellowship for him at an American hospital.
   B. He convinced Carlos to move to New York.
   C. He taught him the heart surgery procedure that made Carlos famous.
   D. He found an apartment for him in New York.

14. **Why did her parents beat Yolanda when she was young?**
   A. She showed the General next door Papi's gun.
   B. She told a neighbor a story about Papi having a gun.
   C. She fired a gun into the coal shed.
   D. She hid Papi's gun in a closet.

15. **Why does Carla go to a different school from her sisters when she first moves to New York?**
   A. She's frightened of the other school.
   B. It's closer to her house.
   C. She doesn't get along with her sisters.
   D. She doesn't want to be in the same grade as Sandi.

16. **What do the Garcia sisters call their Dominican cousins?**
   A. The chaperoned crowd
   B. The Island crowd
   C. The hair-and-nails crowd
   D. The gossip-and-boys crowd

17. **What does Sandi see Mrs. Fanning do outside the bathroom?**
   A. She kisses Carlos on the lips.
   B. She falls over because she's so drunk.
   C. She pulls her skirt up accidentally.
   D. She tries to go into the men's bathroom.

18. **Who is La Bruja?**
   A. A maid who practices voodoo and summons spirits on the Island
   B. A spirit who lives in the haunted coal shed.
   C. The bigoted woman who lives below the Garcias in New York
   D. It's the nickname for the girls' grandmother

19. What is the code word Victor uses?
A. tennis shoes
B. baseball
C. golf ball
D. trouble with a capital T

20. Who is Dona Tatica?
A. One of the Garcia girls' aunts
B. A madam at the brothel Victor visits
C. Don Jose's wife who teaches art
D. A friendly neighbor in New York

21. What are the names of the SIM thugs who interrogate Laura?
A. Pupo and Fabio
B. Pupo and Checo
C. Fabio and Chino
D. Checo and Vic

22. How does Victor know Tio Mundo?
A. They met through a resistance leader in the Dominican Republic
B. They both attended Yale
C. They trained for the CIA together
D. They both attended Harvard

23. Who is Chucha?
A. A Dominican maid who doesn't get along with the other maids
B. One of the Garcia girls' cousins
C. A Haitian laundry maid who practices voodoo and ran away from the family
D. A Haitian maid who practices voodoo and raised Laura

24. What was the name of the Haitian maid who stole clothing and ran away?
A. Gladys
B. Pila
C. Nivea
D. Chucha

25. **Why does Gladys leave the family's service?**
   A. She is rude to them and doesn't work.
   B. She is moving to New York.
   C. They think she stole the mechanical Virgin Mary bank.
   D. They think she'll find a better job.

Quiz 3 Answer Key

1. **(B)** The Prado in Spain
2. **(B)** A naked man with a chain around his neck, sculpting the Virgin Mary.
3. **(B)** Mundin
4. **(D)** He's worried that the children have told about his pornographic magazine.
5. **(B)** He has a post with the United Nations
6. **(C)** They think she is too educated to marry
7. **(C)** He paints sneakers red with nailpolish.
8. **(B)** She doesn't have a favorite toy.
9. **(B)** A CIA agent in the Dominican Republic.
10. **(C)** Sofia was caught going off alone with her boyfriend.
11. **(D)** Sofia
12. **(A)** Chapita
13. **(A)** He secured a fellowship for him at an American hospital.
14. **(B)** She told a neighbor a story about Papi having a gun.
15. **(D)** She doesn't want to be in the same grade as Sandi.
16. **(C)** The hair-and-nails crowd
17. **(A)** She kisses Carlos on the lips.
18. **(C)** The bigoted woman who lives below the Garcias in New York
19. **(A)** tennis shoes
20. **(B)** A madam at the brothel Victor visits
21. **(B)** Pupo and Checo
22. **(B)** They both attended Yale
23. **(D)** A Haitian maid who practices voodoo and raised Laura
24. **(B)** Pila
25. **(C)** They think she stole the mechanical Virgin Mary bank.

Quiz 4

1. **Why did Chucha come to Papito's house?**
    A. She had been chased out of her last employment by anti-Haitian bigots
    B. She was selling silverware and plates, and Papito thought she was very intelligent
    C. She sought asylum after surviving a massacre of Haitians
    D. She was visiting houses to clean them of evil spirits

2. **What is the name of Papi's office in New York?**
    A. Brooklyn Central Clinic
    B. Centro de Medicina
    C. Medicina del Bronx
    D. Medicina para todos

3. **Why is Carla afraid to go to school when she first moves to the States?**
    A. Boys on the playground taunt and molest her.
    B. She doesn't speak English so the teachers think she's stupid.
    C. She is embarrassed by her father's old fashioned appearance when he drives her to school.
    D. She is afraid of taking the bus by herself.

4. **How many children does Sofia have?**
    A. 0
    B. 1
    C. 2
    D. 3

5. **What book does Mamita buy Yolanda?**
    A. The Bible
    B. Discovering Our Bodies
    C. The Divine Comedy
    D. The Arabian Nights

6. **What does Mundin want in return for his pink clay?**
    A. He wants Yolanda to show him that she's a girl
    B. He wants to kiss Yolanda
    C. He wants Yolanda's Human Body doll
    D. He wants her to take the blame for scaring Fifi and Carmencita

7. **Why is the coal shed haunted?**
   A. Pila, a laundry maid, told the children that spirits lived there
   B. Chucha conducts seances there
   C. Going there gives Yolanda nightmares
   D. Yolanda saw a ghost there

8. **What property is adjacent to Papito's?**
   A. Trujillo's estate
   B. A wealthy banker's estate
   C. U.N. Dominican heaquarters
   D. The estate of Trujillo's daughter

9. **What is Sofia's son's name?**
   A. Mundin Carlos
   B. Manuel Gustavo
   C. Carlos Elmenhurst
   D. Carlos Garcia

10. **What is Gladys's dream?**
    A. To marry Carlos Garcia
    B. To become a saint
    C. To be a famous actress in New York
    D. To be a famous musician in New York

11. **What reason does Yolanda give for divorcing John?**
    A. "He is to methodical and rigid."
    B. "He wasn't in love with me."
    C. "We didn't speak the same language."
    D. "I'm in love with Doc instead."

12. **How does Yolanda meet Rudy Elmenhurst?**
    A. They meet at a poetry reading.
    B. He's one of Fifi's ex-boyfriends.
    C. They meet at a party.
    D. They take a poetry class together.

13. **Why does Yolanda throw Rudy out when he visits her during graduate school?**
    A. He only wants to talk about himself.
    B. He just wants to sleep with her.
    C. He accuses her of leading him on.
    D. He tries to spray expensive wine at her.

14. **Why do the girls "rev up" whenever they discuss Manuel Gustavo?**
    A. He drives a flashy car.
    B. He reminds them of a car associated with sleazy, macho men
    C. They catch him and Sofia having sex in a car at a motel.
    D. He uses an electric shaver that makes a "rrrmmm" sound

15. **What sort of poems does Yolanda often write?**
    A. Poems about sex
    B. Poems about her family
    C. Poems that rhyme
    D. Poems about wild animals

16. **How does Laura spend her time after she stops inventing?**
    A. She keeps the accounts and cleans at Carlos's office in the Bronx.
    B. She spends most of the day talking on the phone with her sisters.
    C. She teaches Spanish at a local school.
    D. She works as a receptionist at Carlos's office in the Bronx.

17. **For what occasion is Yolanda asked to write a speech in ninth grade?**
    A. International Students Day
    B. Heritage Day
    C. Teacher's Day
    D. National Poetry Day

18. **Why is Carla confused by the sign "Private, No Tresspassing"?**
    A. She thinks "Private" refers to a soldier in the army
    B. She thinks "tresspassing" is an invented word.
    C. She thinks "tresspassing" is the name of a princess in a storybook she read.
    D. She thinks "tresspassing" refers to doing evil, as in the Lord's Prayer

19. What poem does Yolanda recite on a New York bus?

    A. "The Raven"

    B. "Bedroom Sestina"

    C. "Annabel Lee"

    D. "Thirteen Ways of Looking at a Blackbird"

20. Why does Dr. Fanning get upset at his wife at the restaurant?

    A. She is drinking too much.

    B. She kissed Carlos.

    C. She talks too much.

    D. She is rude to Laura Garcia.

21. What job does Dr. Fanning suggest for Carlos?

    A. General surgeon at a local hospital.

    B. A house doctor at an important hotel.

    C. House doctor at a senior citizens home.

    D. Manager of a Spanish-speaking medicine clinic.

22. What does Carlos say to his new grandson?

    A. He lists famous men who were half-Spanish, half-German

    B. He lists famous chemists

    C. He lists famous men named Charles

    D. He lists his own ancestors

23. Where does Chucha sleep?

    A. With the other maids

    B. Outside

    C. In the sisters' room, to keep watch over them

    D. In her coffin

24. Who is Chino?

    A. A Chinese man who recently moved near the Garcias

    B. One of the SIM thugs who interrogates Laura.

    C. One of the Garcia girls' uncles

    D. A servant that the Garcia family trusts deeply.

25. **What happens to Sandi when she breaks her arm?**
    A. She grows plump because she can't move around much
    B. She begins to draw all the time
    C. She is pampered and becomes dependent on her mother
    D. Her cousins pity her and so buy her ice cream every day

Quiz 4 Answer Key

1. **(C)** She sought asylum after surviving a massacre of Haitians
2. **(B)** Centro de Medicina
3. **(A)** Boys on the playground taunt and molest her.
4. **(C)** 2
5. **(D)** The Arabian Nights
6. **(A)** He wants Yolanda to show him that she's a girl
7. **(A)** Pila, a laundry maid, told the children that spirits lived there
8. **(D)** The estate of Trujillo's daughter
9. **(D)** Carlos Garcia
10. **(C)** To be a famous actress in New York
11. **(C)** "We didn't speak the same language."
12. **(D)** They take a poetry class together.
13. **(B)** He just wants to sleep with her.
14. **(B)** He reminds them of a car associated with sleazy, macho men
15. **(A)** Poems about sex
16. **(A)** She keeps the accounts and cleans at Carlos's office in the Bronx.
17. **(C)** Teacher's Day
18. **(D)** She thinks "tresspassing" refers to doing evil, as in the Lord's Prayer
19. **(C)** "Annabel Lee"
20. **(A)** She is drinking too much.
21. **(B)** A house doctor at an important hotel.
22. **(C)** He lists famous men named Charles
23. **(D)** In her coffin
24. **(D)** A servant that the Garcia family trusts deeply.
25. **(C)** She is pampered and becomes dependent on her mother

ClassicNotes

GradeSaver™

Getting you the grade since 1999™

Other ClassicNotes from GradeSaver™

1984
Absalom, Absalom
Adam Bede
The Adventures of Augie
    March
The Adventures of
    Huckleberry Finn
The Adventures of Tom
    Sawyer
The Aeneid
Agamemnon
The Age of Innocence
The Alchemist (Coelho)
The Alchemist (Jonson)
Alice in Wonderland
All My Sons
All Quiet on the Western
    Front
All the King's Men
All the Pretty Horses
Allen Ginsberg's Poetry
The Ambassadors
American Beauty
And Then There Were
    None
Angela's Ashes
Animal Farm
Anna Karenina
Anthem
Antigone
Antony and Cleopatra
Aristotle's Ethics
Aristotle's Poetics
Aristotle's Politics
As I Lay Dying
As You Like It

Astrophil and Stella
Atlas Shrugged
Atonement
The Awakening
Babbitt
The Bacchae
Bartleby the Scrivener
The Bean Trees
The Bell Jar
Beloved
Benito Cereno
Beowulf
Bhagavad-Gita
Billy Budd
Black Boy
Bleak House
Bless Me, Ultima
Blindness
Blood Wedding
The Bloody Chamber
Bluest Eye
The Bonfire of the
    Vanities
The Book of the Duchess
    and Other Poems
The Book Thief
Brave New World
Breakfast at Tiffany's
Breakfast of Champions
The Brief Wondrous Life
    of Oscar Wao
The Brothers Karamazov
The Burning Plain and
    Other Stories
A Burnt-Out Case
By Night in Chile

Call of the Wild
Candide
The Canterbury Tales
Cat on a Hot Tin Roof
Cat's Cradle
Catch-22
The Catcher in the Rye
The Caucasian Chalk
    Circle
Charlotte Temple
Charlotte's Web
The Cherry Orchard
The Chocolate War
The Chosen
A Christmas Carol
Christopher Marlowe's
    Poems
Chronicle of a Death
    Foretold
Civil Disobedience
Civilization and Its
    Discontents
A Clockwork Orange
Coleridge's Poems
The Color of Water
The Color Purple
Comedy of Errors
Communist Manifesto
A Confederacy of
    Dunces
Confessions
Connecticut Yankee in
    King Arthur's Court
The Consolation of
    Philosophy
Coriolanus

For our full list of over 250 Study Guides, Quizzes,
Sample College Application Essays, Literature Essays and E-texts, visit:

www.gradesaver.com

ClassicNotes

GradeSaver™

Getting you the grade since 1999™

Other ClassicNotes from GradeSaver™

I Know Why the Caged
  Bird Sings
I, Claudius
An Ideal Husband
Iliad
The Importance of Being
  Earnest
In Cold Blood
In Our Time
In the Time of the
  Butterflies
Inherit the Wind
An Inspector Calls
Interpreter of Maladies
Into the Wild
Invisible Man
The Island of Dr. Moreau
Jane Eyre
Jazz
The Jew of Malta
Joseph Andrews
The Joy Luck Club
Julius Caesar
The Jungle
Jungle of Cities
Kama Sutra
Kate Chopin's Short
  Stories
Kidnapped
King Lear
King Solomon's Mines
The Kite Runner
Last of the Mohicans
Leaves of Grass
The Legend of Sleepy
  Hollow

A Lesson Before Dying
Leviathan
Libation Bearers
Life is Beautiful
Life of Pi
Light In August
Like Water for Chocolate
The Lion, the Witch and
  the Wardrobe
Little Women
Lolita
Long Day's Journey Into
  Night
Look Back in Anger
Lord Jim
Lord of the Flies
The Lord of the Rings:
  The Fellowship of the
  Ring
The Lord of the Rings:
  The Return of the
  King
The Lord of the Rings:
  The Two Towers
A Lost Lady
The Lottery and Other
  Stories
Love in the Time of
  Cholera
The Love Song of J.
  Alfred Prufrock
The Lovely Bones
Lucy
Macbeth
Madame Bovary
Maestro

Maggie: A Girl of the
  Streets and Other
  Stories
Manhattan Transfer
Mankind: Medieval
  Morality Plays
Mansfield Park
The Marrow of Tradition
The Master and
  Margarita
MAUS
The Mayor of
  Casterbridge
Measure for Measure
Medea
Merchant of Venice
Metamorphoses
The Metamorphosis
Middlemarch
A Midsummer Night's
  Dream
Moby Dick
A Modest Proposal and
  Other Satires
Moll Flanders
Mother Courage and Her
  Children
Mrs. Dalloway
Much Ado About
  Nothing
My Antonia
Mythology
The Namesake
Native Son

For our full list of over 250 Study Guides, Quizzes,
Sample College Application Essays, Literature Essays and E-texts, visit:

www.gradesaver.com

ClassicNotes

Getting you the grade since 1999™

Other ClassicNotes from GradeSaver™

Nickel and Dimed: On (Not) Getting By in America
Night
Nine Stories
No Exit
Northanger Abbey
Notes from Underground
O Pioneers
The Odyssey
Oedipus Rex or Oedipus the King
Of Mice and Men
The Old Man and the Sea
Oliver Twist
On Liberty
On the Road
One Day in the Life of Ivan Denisovich
One Flew Over the Cuckoo's Nest
One Hundred Years of Solitude
Oroonoko
Oryx and Crake
Othello
Our Town
The Outsiders
Pale Fire
Pamela: Or Virtue Rewarded
Paradise Lost
A Passage to India
The Pearl
Percy Shelley: Poems

Perfume: The Story of a Murderer
Persepolis: The Story of a Childhood
Persuasion
Phaedra
Phaedrus
The Piano Lesson
The Picture of Dorian Gray
Poe's Poetry
Poe's Short Stories
Poems of W.B. Yeats: The Rose
Poems of W.B. Yeats: The Tower
The Poems of William Blake
The Poetry of Robert Frost
The Poisonwood Bible
Pope's Poems and Prose
Portrait of the Artist as a Young Man
Pride and Prejudice
The Prince
The Professor's House
Prometheus Bound
Pudd'nhead Wilson
Pygmalion
Rabbit, Run
A Raisin in the Sun
The Real Life of Sebastian Knight
Rebecca

The Red Badge of Courage
The Remains of the Day
The Republic
Rhinoceros
Richard II
Richard III
The Rime of the Ancient Mariner
Rip Van Winkle and Other Stories
The Road
Robinson Crusoe
Roll of Thunder, Hear My Cry
Romeo and Juliet
A Room of One's Own
A Room With a View
A Rose For Emily and Other Short Stories
Rosencrantz and Guildenstern Are Dead
Salome
The Scarlet Letter
The Scarlet Pimpernel
The Seagull
Season of Migration to the North
Second Treatise of Government
The Secret Life of Bees
The Secret River
Secret Sharer
Sense and Sensibility
A Separate Peace

For our full list of over 250 Study Guides, Quizzes,
Sample College Application Essays, Literature Essays and E-texts, visit:

www.gradesaver.com

ClassicNotes

Gr\deSaver™

Getting you the grade since 1999™

Other ClassicNotes from GradeSaver™

Shakespeare's Sonnets
Shantaram
Short Stories of Ernest
  Hemingway
Short Stories of F. Scott
  Fitzgerald
Siddhartha
Silas Marner
Sir Gawain and the
  Green Knight
Sister Carrie
Six Characters in Search
  of an Author
Slaughterhouse Five
Snow Falling on Cedars
The Social Contract
Something Wicked This
  Way Comes
Song of Roland
Song of Solomon
Songs of Innocence and
  of Experience
Sons and Lovers
The Sorrows of Young
  Werther
The Sound and the Fury
The Spanish Tragedy
Spenser's Amoretti and
  Epithalamion
Spring Awakening
The Stranger
A Streetcar Named
  Desire
Sula
The Sun Also Rises
Tale of Two Cities

The Taming of the Shrew
The Tempest
Tender is the Night
Tess of the D'Urbervilles
Their Eyes Were
  Watching God
Things Fall Apart
The Things They Carried
A Thousand Splendid
  Suns
The Threepenny Opera
Through the Looking
  Glass
Thus Spoke Zarathustra
The Time Machine
Titus Andronicus
To Build a Fire
To Kill a Mockingbird
To the Lighthouse
The Tortilla Curtain
Touching Spirit Bear
Treasure Island
Trifles
Troilus and Cressida
Tropic of Cancer
Tropic of Capricorn
Tuesdays With Morrie
The Turn of the Screw
Twelfth Night
Twilight
Ulysses
Uncle Tom's Cabin
Utopia
Vanity Fair
A Very Old Man With
  Enormous Wings

Villette
The Visit
Volpone
Waiting for Godot
Waiting for Lefty
Walden
Washington Square
The Waste Land
The Wealth of Nations
Where the Red Fern
  Grows
White Fang
A White Heron and
  Other Stories
White Noise
White Teeth
Who's Afraid of Virginia
  Woolf
Wide Sargasso Sea
Wieland
Winesburg, Ohio
The Winter's Tale
The Woman Warrior
Wordsworth's Poetical
  Works
Woyzeck
A Wrinkle in Time
Wuthering Heights
The Yellow Wallpaper
Yonnondio: From the
  Thirties
Zeitoun

For our full list of over 250 Study Guides, Quizzes,
Sample College Application Essays, Literature Essays and E-texts, visit:

www.gradesaver.com

Made in the USA
Lexington, KY
11 December 2017